A HANDBOOK
FOR INTELLIGENCE
AND CRIME ANALYSIS

DAVID
CARIENS

HighTide
Publications, Inc.

Deltaville, Virginia

Copyright © 2016 by David Cariens.

All rights reserved. No part of this publication may be reproduced, distributed or transmitted in any form or by any means, including photocopying, recording, or other electronic or mechanical methods, without the prior written permission of the publisher, except in the case of brief quotations embodied in critical reviews and certain other noncommercial uses permitted by copyright law. For permission requests, write to the publisher, addressed "Attention: Permissions Coordinator," at the address below.

High Tide Publications, Inc.
1000 Bland Point Road
Deltaville, Virginia 23043
www.HighTidePublications.com

Ordering Information: Quantity sales. Special discounts are available on quantity purchases by corporations, associations, and others. For details, contact the "Special Sales Department" at the address above.

Printed in the United States of America

ISBN: 978-0692608548

REF028000 REFERENCE / Handbooks & Manuals
REF026000 REFERENCE / Writing Skills

POL050000POLITICAL SCIENCE /
Public   Policy / Communication Policy

Note to Readers

All statements of fact, opinion, or analysis expressed in this book are those of the author and do not reflect the official positions or views of the Central Intelligence Agency (CIA) or any other U.S. Government agency. Nothing in the contents should be construed as asserting or implying U.S. Government authentication or information or CIA endorsement of the author's views. This book and its contents have been reviewed by the CIA to prevent the disclosure of classified information.

Contents

Introduction

The genesis for the book comes from both ongoing training of intelligence analysts and the problems they encounter in mastering the intelligence style. I have also addressed the problems managers and trainers of intelligence report. Three problems repeatedly come up for producers of finished intelligence:

The first is to conceptualize the reason for writing; why does the analyst want a busy consumer to take time to read what has been written.

The second is the failure of intelligence analysts to challenge their assumptions and therefore build an analytic line based upon false assumptions.

The third is the tendency to write in an academic, not intelligence, style.

The danger of politicization of intelligence is also a major reason for this book. The desire on the part of both consumers and intelligence officers to skew intelligence to fit a given philosophy, bias, or prejudice has increased. I believe this threat to the integrity of intelligence has reached epidemic proportions. The problem is so great that the first chapter deals with politicization.

Chapter 1

The Politicization Of Intelligence

"In the final analysis, the only protections against politicization are the integrity and honesty of the intelligence analysts themselves and the institution of competitive analysis to serve as a safeguard against unchallenged acceptance of conventional wisdom."

Melvin A. Goodman,
National Insecurity, The Cost of American Militarism

The original intent of the book was to be more of a workbook following my earlier textbook on intelligence and crime analysis. But the more I teach intelligence analysts and see the news pundits, the more I read the bias products of so called "think tanks," the more alarmed I am about the integrity of the intelligence profession. And yes, intelligence is a profession; it is not, as some politicians say, a business. The minute the intelligence profession is turned into a business; the minute the need to make a profit takes precedent over the production of objective intelligence, our society is mortally wounded and becomes vulnerable to enemies from both within and without.

All politicians and policy makers want intelligence to support their bias, prejudice, views, and policies. There is nothing wrong with politicians looking to intelligence to support their positions. They all do it—Republicans, Democrats, Tea Party adherents, and libertarians alike. But what is unpardonable is for them to distort, and lie about the facts in order to sell their position. "When the CIA refused to distort the intelligence to suit the conclusions the George W. Bush administration was seeking, the Office of Special Plans was created at the Pentagon under associates of Dick Cheney such as Douglas Feith, William Luti, and Abram Shulsky with the task of making the case for the war against Iraq." (Goodman page 23)

Manipulation of intelligence reached epidemic proportions in the first decade of this century when the United States fought an unnecessary war in Iraq based on unscrupulous manipulation of facts and evidence at the highest levels of the American government.

Even when you are right you are wrong. Following the admission and finger pointing that the case for war against Saddam Hussein's Iraq was based on faulty intelligence, members of the Bush administration neglected to point out the National Intelligence Estimate (NIE) of October 2002 contained dissenting positions; one from the Department of State and the other from Air Force Intelligence. Both undermined the urgency of the need to go to war against Iraq; Colin Powell ignored this information when he addressed the United Nations urging support for military action against Saddam Hussein (a tyrant, but a tyrant with no ties to al Qa'eda).

The Department of State's Bureau of Intelligence and Research (INR) objection read:

State/INR Alternative View of Iraq's Nuclear Program

The Assistant Secretary of State for Intelligence and Research (INR) believes that Saddam continues to want nuclear weapons and that available evidence indicates that Baghdad is pursuing at least a limited effort to maintain and acquire nuclear-related capabilities. The activities we have detected do not, however, add up to a compelling case that Iraq is currently pursuing what INR would consider being an integrated and comprehensive approach to acquire nuclear weapons.

Iraq may be doing so, but INR considers the available evidence inadequate to support such a judgment. Lacking persuasive evidence that Baghdad has launched a coherent effort to reconstitute its nuclear program, INR is unwilling to speculate that such an effort began soon after the departure of UN inspectors or to project a timeline for the completion of activities it does not now see happening. As a result, INR is unable to predict when Iraq could acquire a nuclear device or weapons.

In INR's view Iraq's efforts to acquire aluminum tubes is central to the argument that Baghdad is reconstituting its nuclear weapons program; but INR is not persuaded that the tubes in question are intended for use as centrifuge rotors. INR accepts the judgment of technical experts at the U.S. Department of Energy (DOE) who have concluded that the tubes Iraq seeks to acquire are poorly suited for use in gas centrifuges to be used for uranium enrichment and finds unpersuasive the arguments advanced by others to make the case that they are intended for that purpose. INR considers it far more likely that the tubes are intended for another purpose, most likely the production of artillery rockets. The very large quantities being sought, the way the tubes were tested by the Iraqis, and the atypical lack of attention to operational security in the procurement efforts are among the factor, in addition to the DOE assessment that lead INR to conclude that the tubes are not intended for use in Iraq's nuclear weapon program.

Like a good soldier, Colin Powell saluted and made no reference to his own intelligence unit's disagreement with the NIE.

If the views and objections of the State Department's intelligence unit were not enough to soften the drums of war, then the INR's views combined with those of the Director, Intelligence, Surveillance, and Reconnaissance, US Air Force, produced enough intelligence analysis to cast doubt on the immediacy of the need for war.

Here is the U.S. Air Force, Director, Intelligence, Surveillance and Reconnaissance position:

The Director, Intelligence, Surveillance, and Reconnaissance, US Air Force, does not agree that Iraq is developing UAVs (Unmanned Aerial Vehicles) primarily intended to be delivery platforms for chemical and biological warfare (CBW) agents. The small size of Iraq's new UAV strongly suggests a primary role of reconnaissance, although CBW delivery is an inherent capability.

Those who were hell bent on invading Iraq had two insidious allies—ignorance and laziness. Few in Congress who voted for war knew or questioned the situation. Some, including then- Senator Hilary Clinton, admitted she never read the Key Judgments of the NIE containing the positions of INR and a component of U.S. Air Force intelligence.

The manipulation of intelligence and the fact key members of the Bush administration distorted intelligence and, in so doing, deceived the American public, is unconscionable—but not new.

Others have distorted intelligence. For example, the Gulf of Tonkin Resolution, which gave the Johnson administration a blank check to pursue the Vietnam War, was based on intentional misreading of intelligence.

The George W. Bush administration's deceitfulness in making the case for a decade-long, unnecessary war is the one of the worst cases of politicization of intelligence in the history of this nation. Furthermore, most members of the Senate and House listen to the lobbyists and influence peddlers among their constituents. They fail to brush up on the complexities of foreign policy issues they deal with—particularly the Middle East.

Members of Congress rarely do their own work. They are too busy raising money and trying to get re-elected. They rely on staff members to brief them, and often do not have the intellectual curiosity to investigate or research a problem on their own. And, on those rare occasions when our legislators do take the initiative to delve into complex problems on their own they are unable to act with integrity if their findings do not support the positions of their respective parties, or fit their own bias or prejudice.

Attempts to manipulate and distort intelligence have been around as long as the profession itself. But, with the sharp polarization of the American body politic, efforts to distort, twist, and manipulate intelligence have reached epidemic proportions. Politicization may have already done irrevocable damage to the United States' reputation, economy, and its fighting men and women. The motivator for war in Iraq was not intelligence or Iraq's so-called ties to al Qa'eda; the motivator was ideology and greed—the desire of some in the Bush administration to get hands on Iraq's oil. The war cost the lives of 4,474 American servicewomen and men and wounded another 32,226. This latter figure does not begin to approach the number of men and women who came back from Iraq less than whole; it does not capture the number of servicemen and women who have committed suicide.

Pro-war pundits gloss over one of the most shameless figures of all-the number of civilian casualties. Press reports indicate between 116,000 and 125,000 innocent Iraqi civilians lost their lives; the repulsive euphemism for this is "collateral damage." Military intelligence officers returning from Iraq, who attended my classes between 2008 and 2009, told me the number of civilian casualties was far higher—somewhere between 200,000 and 250,000. Saddam Hussein killed between 250,000 and 500,000 civilians during his 24-year reign of terror—we may have exceeded that figure after six years of war.

All intelligence analysts will face pressure to cook the books at one time or another. Here are some examples:

A few years ago, I taught intelligence analysis and writing to interpreters working alongside our fighting men and women in Afghanistan and Iraq; all of my courses on intelligence analysis contain segments on the importance of the integrity of our profession. An interpreter came up to me at one of our breaks and wanted to discuss a problem he found disturbing. He had translated a document and given it to his supervisor. The supervisor handed it back to him and told him to change the content because the text did not say what he wanted it to say. When the interpreter protested the translation was accurate, the supervisor ordered him to make the change in content or he would "find someone who would."

The problem is obvious—manipulation of raw intelligence. Furthermore, it is indicative of turning intelligence over to private companies who more often than not do not put professional intelligence officers in positions of responsibility. In this case, a $9 billion company had the contract to employ the interpreters. Manipulation of raw intelligence, as cited above, probably led to the loss of American lives just to suit one man's bias and prejudice.

This is just one of several examples I have encountered of deceitful handling of intelligence by people in positions of authority working for major government contractors.

In another instance, an analyst at a different intelligence organization of the Intelligence Community told me an all too familiar story of duplicity. This time it involved an intelligence analyst dealing with international finance. She obtained evidence that high-ranking officials of country "x" were involved in money laundering for terrorist groups, including some planning attacks on U.S. installations and personnel worldwide. The Prime Minister of country "x" was scheduled to make a formal visit to the United States and she wanted to do an intelligence report alerting policy makers of country "x's" officials support of terrorism. Her supervisor would not allow the report to go forward.

As time drew closer and closer for the Prime Minister's visit, the damning evidence continued to mount regarding country "x" officials. Finally, in her frustration, and realizing U.S. lives and property were at stake, she took the evidence around to the head of her unit, insisting the intelligence be produced. She won; the report went out, and U.S. officials put pressure on the Prime Minister of country "x" to stop the money laundering. The pressure worked and al Qa'eda and other terrorists lost an important avenue to finance their operations.

No good deed goes unpunished. The analyst did the right thing and prevailed. However, her immediate supervisor, embarrassed by her actions, never forgave her, and refused to sign off on her promotions. Her career stalled and, in the end, she transferred out of that office.

I had a similar experience. In the early 1980s, the CIA selected me as one of five CIA intelligence analysts to write a paper addressing a key intelligence subject. The papers would become "the CIA's" intelligence position on those subjects.

As an East European specialist, my subject was the prospect for the post-Tito succession in Yugoslavia. The five of us were relocated from our respective offices and put in a separate office especially created for our work.

We all felt as if we had died and gone to analysts' heaven. We were given one year to produce our papers and given a blank check. I was told, if I need to consult with academics anywhere do it—don't ask just go. If I need to attend professional conferences on Eastern Europe and the Balkans—go. The only stipulation was I had to use a methodology tool in my analysis. Methodologies were just coming to the fore and the CIA wanted to demonstrate to Congress and others that it was in the forefront of analytical tools.

I was given indicators of instability as my methodology. I had no training in indicators and warning, but felt the words were self-explanatory. I came up with a list of 26 indicators and color-coded them—green, yellow, and red. Out of the 26 indicators one was red, two were yellow, and 23 were green.

If I were to put the paper's conclusion in one sentence, it would be: "So long as the Soviet Union and Warsaw Pact exist, the Yugoslav federation will remain intact because the constituent republics and provinces see their best chance of a nearly autonomous existence to be within the federation."

When I finished the paper, it went through the obligatory review and editing process before landing on the desk of the Office Chief.

I was called to meet with the Office Chief and what I experienced was something like the Spanish Inquisition.

I was seated on a straight-back wooden chair in front of the Office Chief. To his right was his deputy and to his left was the chief editor. Other members of management were on both sides of him including my immediate supervisor.

He began by saying how well researched and written the paper was—but said he wanted me to change the conclusions. He wanted me to say there was danger of the Yugoslav federation falling apart. The danger of civil war, and bloodshed was likely.

Stunned, I asked him what I had missed? I spent a year of my professional life working on this paper. If I missed important evidence, then I would be disappointed in myself, but would change the paper.

His response was something like this, "Oh you didn't miss anything. I want you change your conclusions; I am telling you to change your conclusions." I objected, saying I could not do that without the evidence.

At this point the Office Chief became agitated. He then said, "Let me put it this way; if you tell the President and Congress the Yugoslav Federation is going to hold together and there is war and bloodshed within the next six-to-twelve months, that is bad for your career, and it is bad for my career. Now, if you do as I say and tell policy makers there is a strong likelihood of civil war and bloodshed and nothing happens, that is good for your career and good for my career."

I suffer from acute foot-in-mouth disease and as soon as he finished I shot back, "If that is the kind of intelligence analysis you want, I suggest you go to my sons' high school in Fairfax County, but I doubt you will get it because the school is reputable.

Furthermore, if you put the paper out, take my name off of it. If it is published the way you want, I will be on the phone to every member of the Intelligence Community I deal with telling them what happened in this room." I got up and walked out of my room, followed by my supervisor telling me to calm down.

In the hallway outside, my supervisor told me I misunderstood—the paper would be published. I responded, "Fine, the paper will go out as I wrote it." He replied, "No, we will have to change the conclusions."

I just turned and walked away.

All of you who work in bureaucracies know that within minutes the news there had been a big blow-up over the Yugoslav paper spread throughout the Intelligence Directorate. I became a nonperson. People were reluctant to be seen with me.

About two weeks went by before I heard the Deputy Director for Intelligence asked to see the paper exactly the way the analyst had written it. My career was dead in the water when I balked at the changes. I was now sinking.

It got worse.

The Deputy Director liked the paper and ordered my version be printed. Remember, no good deed goes unpunished. My career was sunk because I challenged the equivalent of a one-star general and won. He would never forgive me.

Unfortunately, what I classified as bad continued to get worse. The paper was cabled out through secure channels to Ambassador Lawrence Eagleburger in Belgrade. The Ambassador loved the paper, and cabled back to tell the Agency it was one of the best and well-written products he had seen on Yugoslavia.

Guess who was the first person to congratulate me on Eagleburger's comments? The horse's rear end who wanted me to change the conclusions. Now, he could say that under his careful guidance the analyst had been able to produce the paper.

I was not forgiven, and ended up transferring out of the office in order to get away from the Office Chief's vindictiveness. Ironically, I can thank the man for opening up a great opportunity to me—teaching intelligence analysis and training new analysts.

My story is very mild. No lives were at stake. What was at stake was the integrity of our profession. Once intelligence analysts lose their objectivity and integrity, they might as well pack up, go home, and stop wasting the taxpayers' money. Everywhere I go to teach, when I tell the story, analysts and officers tell me what happened to them. Whether it is an Arizona State Police officer who was told to lie (and would not) in court because the evidence did not fit the prosecuting attorney's theory of the case, or the Royal Canadian Mounted Police (RCMP) officer who told me he was told to drop an investigation involving the murder of a fellow police officer— the implication being it was not politically wise to proceed.

A few years ago, I was teaching a group of twelve intelligence officers from the National Counterterrorism Center (NCTC). In the class was a man in his late 30s who was a former history professor at a university in Florida. At one point, when we were discussing the ethics of the profession, he announced to the class in no uncertain terms that intelligence should always fit and support policy makers. I wanted to ask him at which university had he taught because I never want a family member to attend that school. I didn't, but did stress with him the importance of objectivity and the need for all intelligence analysts to leave their political and personal views outside the office in the pursuit of objectivity.

There is another danger analysts face and that is falling in love with your account or problem. I was a Yugoslav analyst much of my career. It was fun to write intelligence about Yugoslavia when their leadership was sticking it to the Soviets, but when the Yugoslavs did the same thing to the U.S., I had to be careful not to write intelligence explaining away Belgrade's actions or making excuses.

The stories go on and on.

Efforts to manipulate intelligence are omnipresent. Sometimes people's actions are overt and malicious. They have agendas they will pursue at all costs no matter how many lives are lost or how much money is squandered. Sometimes manipulation is subliminal, particularly on the part of analysts who are looking for evidence to support their theories or analysis and find ways to disregard or explain away evidence that does not.

The rest of this book will deal with the practical aspects of writing intelligence analysis. As an analyst, you will be required to sweat intellectual blood in tackling complicated problems and situations. You will have fragmentary facts and evidence, yet you will be required to make analytical conclusions, and put those conclusions in a form of English readily understandable in one reading—*and*, not lose any of the complexity of the subject you are dealing with. That is a daunting task and is why intelligence writing is one of the most difficult forms of writing.

Every intelligence analyst reading this book has or will come under pressure to manipulate intelligence—to cook the books. No matter how well you master the intelligence writing skills spelled out in the following chapters, you will butt heads with consumers in positions of authority who will go to great lengths to discredit your work if it runs counter to their bias, prejudice or views.

The best defense against the manipulation of intelligence is a well reasoned, well researched and a clear and concise intelligence product leaving the reader little or no room to manipulate or distort. And, in a perverse way, if you have achieved excellence in your analytical writing skills, and the reader cannot politicize your work, then he or she will ignore it. There is nothing you can do about that.

Every intelligence analyst needs to be thinking how he or she will handle this problem. Those who politicize are something akin to playground bullies. Playground bullies are not used to having someone stand up to them. Therefore, standing your ground can stop much of the manipulation of intelligence.

The bottom line is all intelligence analysts need to be contemplating ways to improve the integrity of the profession. There are avenues available to all analysts to challenge politicization. The two major ones that come to mind are the Inspector General and the ombudsman.

Now, let's turn our attention to the basic building blocks of intelligence writing—words, sentences, and paragraphs.

Chapter 2

The Basic Building Blocks

Having discussed the politicization of intelligence in detail, the next step is to look at how to prevent this corruption of our profession. The best way to prevent the manipulation of intelligence is to produce well researched, well thought out, and well written intelligence products. Your goal, as an intelligence analyst, should be to produce a product that can be read in one sitting by the consumer, so the reader does not need to stop or pause as he or she reads the product.

Some critics of intelligence scoff at our products, saying the intelligence is the analyst's or organization's opinion. Nothing could be further from the truth. Here are definitions of "an opinion" and "an analytic judgment."

Opinion	An opinion is a statement of preference whose grounds are wholly personal
Analytical Judgment	An analytical judgment is one whose grounds of support do not depend on the individual who holds them

Our intelligence products stand on the merits of the evidence and the logic of our arguments. Our personal feelings or opinions should never enter into our analysis.

The intelligence must be clear and concise. In the final analysis, you should strive to make your written product so well argued and documented that it cannot be distorted. Intelligence writing is simple, but not simplistic. You cannot make anyone read or believe what you have written if it runs counter to deeply ingrained beliefs or prejudices, but you can make it next to impossible to distort what you have written. If you have done that, and the consumer rejects your words, he or she will just ignore it and pretend it doesn't exist.

Indeed one of the greatest obstacles we face is to fight ignorance and prejudice against facts and evidence. I am reminded of the reaction of a family member of a student who was killed at the Appalachian School of Law. After reading my book on the law school shooting and the documentation dealing with the incompetence on the part of some people in positions of authority making that shooting inevitable, she said, "The book cannot be true because it's not the way I heard it happened." One of the most difficult things we face is to challenge beliefs and prejudice that place their adherents beyond the reach of every means of persuasion. It does not require any special knowledge of psychology or neuroscience to observe human beings can be stubbornly reluctant to change their minds.

We cannot do much to combat this stubbornness, but we can produce the best intelligence possible given the evidence we compile. So, let's examine the basic building blocks of our trade: words, sentences, and paragraphs.

English

You can put a date on the origins of English as we know it today; an event that played a pivotal role in giving English four characteristics that make it one of the most difficult languages to use correctly. That date is 1066—the Battle of Hastings. The French-speaking Normans crossed the English Channel and conquered the Anglo-Saxons who spoke a mostly Germanic language. The mixing of the two peoples and languages began. As a result, at the heart of modern English are two core sets of words: The one and two syllable words of the farmer, blacksmith, and man and woman trying to eke out a living, and the multi- syllable words brought in by the nobles. The latter, more often than not, deal with complicated and sophisticated ideas. The outcome of this mixing of the two languages has resulted in four characteristics that make correct use of English so difficult:

First, English is not phonetic—you cannot spell words based on the way you pronounce them.

Second, in English a rule is not a rule; a rule is a suggestion.

Third, English often defies logic.

Fourth, English grammar and punctuation looks simple, but in fact are difficult because there are often as many exceptions to a rule as there are adherents.

Now, let's take a closer look at the vocabulary, sentence structure, and paragraph style at the heart of intelligence writing.

Words

Intelligence analysts use simple vocabulary wherever possible. We are not academics; we do not reach for multi-syllable words to show how many degrees we have acquired. Do not reach for the more complicated and sophisticated words if a simple one or two syllable Anglo-Saxon-based word fits. I am not saying don't use multi-syllable words—of course you use them if they are the best fit. Just don't reach for them to try and impress your audience with your vocabulary.

Choosing the right word or words to convey your meaning is essential to improving your writing. Most people use far too many words and in the process introduce confusion and ambiguity into their writing. Remember, once your written work goes to the consumer, you will not be in the room to say, "No, that is not what I meant to say. I meant to say …" The following are some simple rules to help you improve your word choice. Therefore, keep the following in mind:

> Draw on the one and two syllable words in English of Anglo-Saxon origin. These words usually, but not always, have a limited number of meanings and by using them you go a long way toward maintaining clarity.

> Minimize the use of pronouns. The antecedent of a pronoun may not be clear.

> Do not try to impress your audience by looking for multi-syllable words not in common usage in an attempt to send your reader to the dictionary (he or she won't go).

> Avoid using foreign words in your text, unless the foreign word is the precise one you need and there is no English equivalent.

> When writing intelligence do not use the ampersand (&).

Sentences

Grammarians used to say an English sentence must have a subject, verb, and predicate. Now, grammarians have revised their "rule" and say an English sentence must have subject, verb, and complete thought. Ah-h, that is simple and it makes sense. But even this revision is deceptive because complete thought is not the same as understanding. You can understand a sentence fragment; every day each one of us talks and writes in sentence fragments. The problem with a sentence fragment is something is left out. Any time you leave something out of a sentence you invite the reader to fill in.

For intelligence analysts, leaving something out of a sentence can have dire consequences. You are not in the room when the analysis is being read so you can explain what was left out. In the production of intelligence, the failure to use complete sentences can, at minimum, leave the door open for the reader to fill in whatever fits her or his bias or prejudice. Whatever you meant will not be the idea the consumer fills in.

Intelligence uses a lot of simple, active voice sentences as well as complex and compound sentences. Keep in mind intelligence analysts are vying for busy decision makers time; it makes sense to keep the writing simple. In fact, the Intelligence Community in general puts a high premium on sentences with little or no punctuation. So, if you have trouble with English grammar and punctuation, you have found the right profession.

Intelligence writing is clear, concise, expository writing with no frills. We do not deal in nuance or innuendo, nor do we create mood. Intelligence analysts practically eliminate adjectives from their written products. What do adjectives do? They add color and emotion to writing. Adjectives are a main staple of creative and academic writing, but they are the bane of an intelligence analyst's existence because they can, by adding emotion, bring into question the analyst's objectivity. Intelligence analysts also reduce their use of adverbs, if for no other reason than they are over used in writing and add little to the intelligence product. The goal of the intelligence analyst is to make her or his written product understood in one reading, it is therefore simple—but it is not simplistic.

Simple Sentences

Simple sentences are, more often than not, short and to the point. The main thing you want to keep in mind is to avoid unnecessary passive voice sentences. The over use of passive voice is one of the biggest complaints managers have about their analysts' writing. It is an easy problem to fix. If you know the actor, put the actor ahead of the verb. Look at the following unnecessary passive voice:

The bank was robbed by the hole-in-the-wall gang.

The sentence should read:

The-hole-in-the-wall gang robbed the bank.

There is an easy way for you to check yourself for unnecessary passive voice. Before you turn your draft in read through it and circle the word "by" every time you use it. Look at those sentences. Most are probably unnecessary passive voice. Again, remember put the actor in front of the verb to avoid unnecessary passive voice.

Complex Sentences

Complex sentences are the bread and butter of intelligence writing. I define them as a simple sentence with a dependent clause or phrase (grammarians say simple sentence and a dependent clause). Here is an example:

Simple Sentence	Phrase
There will be a coup in Uganda tomorrow,	*according to a reliable source.*

The question is where to put the phrase. There is a general guideline or suggestion when it comes to topic sentences. You put the point you are making (the simple sentence first) and phrase (the source or how you know the assertion you made, second). The idea is nothing should stand between the reader and the point you are making.

However, there are exceptions: If the information is highly questionable, yet the source has been reliable, the source citation should come first. For example, you might see the following:

According to a reliable source, the Queen of England is going to abdicate in favor of her grandson, Prince William.

The above is highly unlikely, but because of the source's reliability, the information should be given serious consideration.

You also put the source citation first if that is the standard template of the intelligence organization employing you. Placing the source citation first is common in some police intelligence reports and some military intelligence reports.

Compound Sentences

Compound sentences are defined as two simple sentences joined by a conjunction. A comma must precede the conjunction. The failure to have a comma in compound sentences is one of the twenty-five most frequent mistakes made in written English. Here is an example of a compound sentence:

I like apples, and I like pears.

Many of your compound sentences will be broken into two simple sentences, especially if a professional intelligence editor is reviewing your work.

Topic Sentences

The topic sentence of the first paragraph is the most important sentence of your whole paper. The topic sentence of each paragraph is the most important sentence of that paragraph. I know you have read that several times already, but it is so important and bears repeating.

The topic sentence must capture the main point of what you are trying to tell the reader. The topic sentence is the hook; it tells the reader why he or she should spend his or her valuable time reading your intelligence.

The topic sentence captures what is going on, or has happened, and what it means. The last part is critical. Intelligence analysts give meaning, definition, or understanding to problems or situations the reader can find nowhere else. The topic sentence of the first paragraph conceptualizes the whole paper. The failure of analysts to do this conceptualization upfront is one of the most serious problems managers have with their intelligence analysts. 1 devote Chapter 3 to conceptualizing the topic sentence.

Paragraphs

The construction of an intelligence paragraph often proves difficult because it flies in the face of most of the writing training we had in academia. The difficulty, in part, stems from the fact that, while the academic and intelligence analyst use the same vocabulary in talking about writing, the words they use have different meanings.

A prime example of this difference is the use of the word "summary" to describe the initial paragraph of a longer paper. There are similarities between the two, but there are important differences.

Here are the similarities:

- Both the academic and intelligence analyst use the summary paragraph to capture the main point or points of a longer piece of work.
- Both the academic and intelligence summaries do not contain any information not in the body of the paper.
- Both the academic and intelligence summaries establish the relationship between the main point and supporting evidence or details.

Here are the differences:

- The intelligence summary gives the reader the main analytic point in the first sentence.
- The academic summary does not put the main point in the topic sentence. If it does, the sentence may begin with a dependent phrase or clause to set the stage (a dependent phrase or clause is rarely used in the topic sentence of an intelligence summary paragraph).
- The intelligence summary adheres to the Inverted Pyramid Paragraph style—going from the overriding most important point—the point of the whole paper, to the least important. The academic summary may or may not be organized from most important to least important.

- The intelligence summary rarely, if ever, contains background information. Academic summary paragraphs frequently contain one or more sentence, phrase, or clause to set the stage or give background.

The success of any intelligence paragraph depends on the strength of the topic sentence. The importance of the topic sentence in intelligence writing cannot be overstated.

Let's take a closer look at that sentence and the Inverted Pyramid Paragraph.

The Inverted Pyramid Paragraph

The Inverted Pyramid Paragraph is the standard form of paragraph writing used throughout the Intelligence Community— when you do not have another template. The Inverted Pyramid Paragraph is based on the paragraphs used by journalists.

An intelligence paragraph needs a clear, single focus. And, as I have said, in intelligence writing the major analytic point is found in the topic sentence and gives meaning to the facts or evidence contained in succeeding sentences.

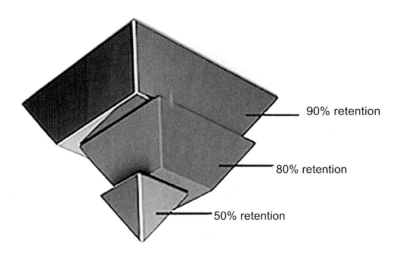

90% retention

80% retention

50% retention

Intelligence analysts prefer the Inverted Pyramid Paragraph because it puts the key point, or analytic point, at the beginning of the paragraph. Research has shown that readers, particularly busy decision makers, skim read. How do you skim read? You read the topic sentence and you remember it. Then your eyes flow over the rest of the paragraph. By putting the main point up front, you ensure that if the reader understands nothing else you have written, he or she will understand the main intelligence (analytic) point you are making.

The journalist tries to get the "who, what, when, where, and why" into the topic sentence. An intelligence analyst tries to get the bottom line up front (BLUF). Another way to say it is the "what or why" he or she is writing and the "so what" into the topic sentence. If any of you have taken courses in intelligence writing you have been exposed to this concept—there are many names for it: "the bottom line up front" (BLUF), "the big picture, bottom line," "the statement of synthesis," "a strong topic sentence," or, as I have said, "the what and the so what." No matter what you call it, we are all talking about the same thing; the need to tell the reader in the first sentence the main reason why you are writing and the significance of your analysis.

The sentences in the rest of the paragraph should be in descending order of importance. In other words, the second sentence should be the most important piece of evidence, contextual data, or fact supporting the analytical point you are making; then the next important and the next important.

The ideal paragraph should be no more than four sentences. This is not a rule; it is a suggestion. Some of you have probably been taught all paragraphs should have at least three sentences— a beginning, a middle, and an end. That is no longer the rule. It is now correct to have a one-sentence paragraph in professional writing. In intelligence writing, a one sentence paragraph often begins the intelligence article—it is the "what or why and so what." Indeed, in some formats, that sentence is printed in bold print to alert the readers that if you don't take anything else away from this intelligence product remember the topic sentence.

The sentences in all paragraphs should move logically from one to another. In intelligence paragraphs, the logic rests on the fact that the information is presented in descending order of importance. The succeeding paragraphs provide evidence, facts or contextual data rated to the point made in the topic sentence.

In intelligence writing it is important you think about the order of your sentences.

Diagram #1
The Inverted Pyramid Paragraph

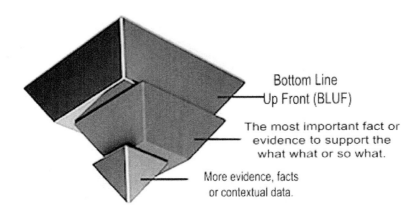

Bottom Line
Up Front (BLUF)

The most important fact or
evidence to support the
what what or so what.

More evidence, facts
or contextual data.

How do you know when you have finished your Inverted Pyramid Paragraph? This is where it gets tricky. You are finished when you have presented the strongest evidence, facts, or contextual data to support your analytical assertion. You do not wrap it up the way you do in traditional paragraph writing. You will feel you are leaving the reader hanging because this was not the way you were taught to write a paragraph. You are not; you are presenting your intelligence analysis in a clear, concise, and visually digestible form for the busy intelligence consumer.

Diagram #2

The Traditional Paragraph

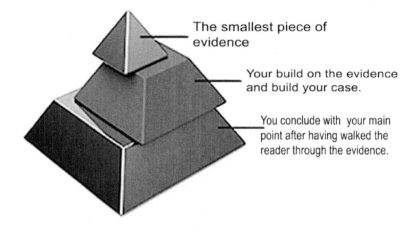

The smallest piece of evidence

Your build on the evidence and build your case.

You conclude with your main point after having walked the reader through the evidence.

The Inverted Pyramid Paragraph is built on the theory intelligence consumers will read and retain 90% of what they read in the topic sentence. Retention drops as the reader goes through the paragraph until, at the last sentence, the percentage that retain the information may drop to 50%. That is not good enough.

Diagram # 3
Multi-Paragraph Intelligence

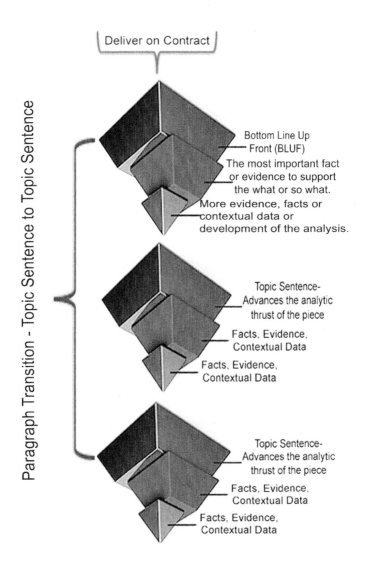

You can see, from the diagrams on the previous pages, how important it is to conceptualize the main analytic point you are making—your reason for writing. That sentence should be the driving force for your paragraph (or paragraphs). The failure of intelligence analysts to make his or her analytic point clear; to show why the subject discussed meets the threshold for the reader's consideration; and to demonstrate why the reader will find analysis in this intelligence product he will find nowhere else, can spell the difference as to whether or not your intelligence will be read.

This lack of conceptualization of the topic sentence is so serious that, after discussing it with training officers at the FBI and CIA, I decided to devote the next chapter to that sentence.

Paragraph Unity

When every sentence in a paragraph contributes to the development of one central idea, the paragraph has unity. If a paragraph contains sentences that do not develop a central idea, then the paragraph lacks unity.

The following is a paragraph from a report in which the possible locations for a new distribution center are evaluated. Does the paragraph have unity?

> *The greatest advantage of Chicago as the location for our new distribution center is its excellent transportation facilities. In fact, Chicago was at one time the hub of cross-country rail transportation. Chicago is also a major center of the trucking industry, and most of the nation's large freight carriers have terminals there. We are concerned, however, about the delivery problems that we've had with several truck carriers. We had far fewer problems with airfreight. Both domestic and international air cargo services are available at O'Hare International Airport. Finally, except in the winter months when the Great Lakes are frozen, Chicago is a seaport, accessible through the St. Lawrence.*

Now read the paragraph after it has been edited for unity. Each of the remaining sentences is directly related to the central idea, and the paragraph has unity.

The greatest advantage of Chicago as the location for our new distribution center is its excellent transportation facilities. The city is served by three major railroads. Chicago is also a major center of the trucking industry, and most of the nation's large freight carriers have terminals there. Both domestic and international air cargo services are available at O'Hare International Airport. Except in the winter months when the Great Lakes are frozen, Chicago is a seaport, accessible through the St. Lawrence Seaway.

Now that we have examined the mechanics of intelligence paragraph construction, we will move on and take a greater look at conceptualization.

Chapter 3

Conceptualization

Before starting this book, I asked managers and trainers of intelligence analysts what they would like the contents to address. Two answers repeatedly came up:

- The need to conceptualize or to know the main analytic point you the analyst want to present.

- The problem of making false assumptions, and then building on those assumptions, with the result of wrong or badly flawed analysis.

Therefore, I am devoting a chapter to each topic. This chapter will deal with conceptualization and the next with assumptions.

Every analyst, indeed every writer, should be able to conceptualize in one sentence what the point is the author wants to get across to the reader. In the case of the intelligence analyst, the ability to capture the readers' attention with a solid intelligence, analytic point in the first sentence may well determine if the paper is read.

The importance of this topic sentence cannot be overstated— the topic sentence will make or break your intelligence product. Nearly all readers of intelligence decide whether or not to continue reading based on the topic sentence. The topic sentence tells the reader why he or she should take time out of his or her busy day and read your intelligence.

Intelligence analysts do not use techniques other writers have. For example, we should not use questions in the title or the topic sentence. Our job is to answer questions, not raise them. We also don't have the option of playing on words to attract the readers' attention. (*The Economist* uses this style.) Plays on words often involve humor, and humor is frowned on in intelligence writing; we are not creative writers, and humor undercuts the seriousness of what we are addressing. We have to be direct and straightforward. A play-on-words often requires the reader to stop and ponder. Our goal is to write paragraphs that can be read straight through without stopping.

I think it is time for an example of what I mean. Please read the article China's New Military on the next six pages and then write, in one sentence, the main intelligence point you want the reader to take away.

China's New Military

By Sedgwich Twiford

The Walla Walla Times-Courier

(Beijing) China has been trying to update its military for more than two decades, attempting to push its low-tech, manpower-heavy force it calls the People's Army into the modern world of computers, satellites, and electronic weapons. U.S. and Taiwanese military officials are concerned about China's rapid development of cruise and other anti-ship missiles designed to pierce the electronic defenses of U.S. vessels that are stationed in the area.

China has taken delivery of two Russian-built Bigski-class missile destroyers and has ordered six more. The destroyers are equipped with Sunburn missiles able to skim 4 and ½ feet above the water and travel a speed of Mach 2.5— enabling them to evade radar detection. China is also buying eight Girggleglub-class submarines that carry Sinkalott anti-ship missiles with a range of 145 miles. Military experts in Taipei say these vessels will present a significant challenge to the U.S. military presence.

The Type-007 nuclear missile submarine, launched last year to replace a trouble-prone Woops-class vessel, can carry 16 intercontinental ballistic missiles. Coupled with the newly developed Juang-2 missile, which has a range of more than 5,000 miles and an ability to carry independently targeted warheads, the Type-007 submarine will give China a survivable nuclear deterrent against the continental United States, according to an article in "Modern Military" by Claus von Burgermeister.

The Dongding-31 solid-fuel mobile ballistic missile, land- based equivalent to the Ying-Yang-2, has been deployed in the last few months to augment the approximately 20 Dongding-5 liquid fuel missiles already in service, according to Pentagon sources.

The Dongding-31 will be joined by an 8,000 mile Dongding-41. Once this deployment takes place the entire United States will be within range of land-based Chinese- based ICBMs.

A Chinese source has been quoted in diplomatic circles as saying these missiles are not meant to attack the United States. They are, however, meant to throw a monkey wrench into decision–making in Washington. The missiles are meant to make the U.S. think twice about many of its decisions and actions regarding Taipei and Beijing.

With a $1.3 trillion economy growing at more than nine percent a year, China has acquired more than enough wealth to make these investments in a modern, state-of-the- art military. China's announced defense budget has risen by double digits in most recent years. Last year it jumped 12.6 percent to over $30 billion.

The Pentagon estimates that real military expenditures, including weapons acquisitions and research into other budgets, should make the defense budget two or three times the announced figure. That figure would make China's defense budget one of the largest in the world, but still far behind the $400 billion spent by the United States.

Taiwan

Taiwan, the self-ruled island that China insists must reunite with the mainland, has long been a center of growth in military spending. One of the Taiwanese military's main goals is to protect the island from invasion by Communist China.

Indeed, mainland China has deployed more than 600 short- range ballistic missiles aimed at Taiwan. These missiles are located in China's Fujian and Jiangxi provinces. Medium- range missiles have also been deployed, and much of Beijing's modernization campaign is directed at acquiring weapons and support systems that would give it air and sea superiority in any conflict over the 100-mile-wide Taiwan Strait.

The expansion of China's interests abroad, particularly energy needs, has also broadened the military's mission in recent years. Increasingly, according to foreign specialists and Chinese commentators, China's navy and air force have set out to project power in the South China Sea, and in the East China Sea, where China and Japan are at loggerheads over mineral rights and several contested islands.

China has acquired signals-monitoring facilities on Myanmar's Coco Island. It also will have similar monitoring facilities at a port it is building in cooperation with Pakistan near the Iranian border at Gwadar. This site looks out over tankers exiting the Persian Gulf.

According to a report prepared for the U.S. Secretary of Defense, China has developed a "string of pearls" strategy, seeking military-related agreements with Bangladesh, Cambodia, and Thailand—in addition to its agreements with Burma and Pakistan.

Against this backdrop, unifying Taiwan with the mainland has become more than just a nationalist goal. The 13,500 square-mile territory has also become a platform that China needs to protect southern sea lanes, through which pass 80 percent of its imported oil and tons of other imported raw materials. It could serve as a base for Chinese submarines to have unfettered access to the deep Pacific, according to Taiwanese military officials. "Taiwan for them now is a strategic must and no longer a sacred mission," a U.S. official is quoted as saying.

Traditionally, China's threat against Taiwan has been seen as a Normandy-style invasion by troops hitting the beaches. Indeed, French, German, British, and Mexican military attaches were invited to observe such landing exercises by special Chinese troops.

Military analysts also note China's fast-pace ship construction program includes landing vessels and troop transports. Two giant transports that were seen under construction in Shanghai's shipyards a year ago, have apparently been launched in preparation for deployment.

U.S. and Taiwanese officials believe that China's amphibious forces have the ability to move only one armored division—12,000 troops and vehicles—across the straits at this time. That would be enough to occupy only some of the outlying islands.

Taiwanese officials said that if a conflict occurs, they expect a graduated campaign of high-tech pinpoint attacks, including cruise missile strikes on key government offices or computer sabotage, designed to force the leadership in Taipei to negotiate and prevent an all-out war. The 1996 crisis, when China test-fired missiles off the coast, cost the Taiwanese $20 billion in lost business and mobilization expenses.

High-Tech Emphasis

A little-discussed but key facet of China's military modernization has been a reduction in personnel and an effort to better train and equip the soldiers who remain, particularly those who operate high-technology weapons. Clyde Finkelbaum, a former U.S. military attaché in Beijing who is writing a book on his experiences in China, said that forming a core of skilled commissioned and noncommissioned officers and other specialists who can make the military run in a high-tech environment may be just as important in the long run as buying sophisticated weapons.

Premier Chung Wong told the National People's Congress recently that his government would soon complete a 200,000-soldier reduction that has been underway for three years. That would leave about 2.3 million troops in the Chinese military, making it still the world's largest, according to a report from the Defense Intelligence Agency.

Because of pensions and retraining for dismissed soldiers, the training and personnel reduction program has so far been an expense rather than a cost-cutter. But it has encountered competition for funds from high-tech and high-expense programs designed to make China's military capable of waging what former President Wee Tu Bad called "war in the modern world."

The emphasis on high-tech warfare, as opposed to China's traditional reliance on masses of ground troops, was dramatized by shifts last September in the Communist Party's decision-making Central Military Commission, which has long been dominated by the People's Liberation Army. Air force commander Ding Chang, Navy commander, Wong Dong, and 2nd Artillery commander Wing Chou, whose units control China's ballistic missiles, joined the commission for the first time, signaling the importance of their responsibilities under the modernization program.

Air Superiority

Striving for air superiority over the Taiwan Strait, the air force has acquired more than 250 Sukhoi Su-27 single-role and Su-30 all-weather, multi-role fighter planes, according to Pentagon sources. The Pentagon has forecast that, as the Sukhoi program continues to add to China's aging inventory, the air force will field about 2,000 planes by 2020, of which about 150 will be fourth-generation craft equipped with sophisticated avionics.

However, specialists noted that many of China's SU-27s have spent most of the time on the ground for lack of maintenance. In addition, according to U.S. and Taiwanese experts, China has remained at the beginning stages in its effort to acquire the equipment and skills necessary for midair refueling, space-based information systems, and airborne reconnaissance and battle management platforms.

A senior Taiwanese military source said Chinese pilots started training on refueling and airborne battle management several years ago, but so far have neither the equipment nor the technique to integrate such operations into their order of battle. Similarly, he said, China has been testing use of Global Positioning Systems to guide its cruise missiles but remains some time away from deploying such technology.

Buying such electronic equipment would be China's most likely objective if the European Union goes ahead with plans to lift its arms sales embargo despite objections from Washington, a senior

European diplomat in Beijing said. A Chinese effort to acquire Israel's Phalcon airborne radar system was stymied in 2000 when the United States prevailed on Israel to back out of a $1 billion deal.

Now, compare what you have written, with the school solution below.

China: Strides In Military Modernization

A top-to-bottom modernization program is transforming the Chinese military, raising the stakes for U.S. forces in the Far East and giving Chinese missiles the capability to strike the U.S.

Once you have looked at the school solution, look at the paragraph that flows from the topic sentence above.

China: Strides In Military Modernization

A top-to-bottom modernization program is transforming the Chinese military, raising the stakes for U.S. forces in the Far East and giving Chinese missiles the capability to strike the U.S. Several programs to improve China's armed forces could soon produce a stronger nuclear deterrent against the United States, soldiers better trained to use high- technology weapons, and more effective cruise and anti-ship missiles for use in and around the Taiwan Straits. China has not developed a weapon system that suddenly changes the balance of power, but Beijing has made major strides forward in its navy through the purchase of submarines and destroyers from the Russians and sophisticated missile development. Beijing sees the military modernization program moving China closer to regaining control over Taiwan.

An important part of conceptualization in intelligence writing is the connection between the title and the topic sentence. In fact, the title and the topic sentence combine to make "the hook" in intelligence writing. Another way to put it is the title is the contract with the reader and the topic sentence delivers on the contract.

How many of you have started to read a newspaper article based on the title only to find out the topic sentence has nothing to do with the title? It gets worse when the whole first paragraph doesn't have the foggiest connection to the title. The result? You stop reading.

Here is a simple formula to help you develop a title that will serve as a contract. Use the name of the geographic area, or topic you are dealing with such as drug trafficking or terrorism. Write that down and put a colon after it. Then, in four or five words say to yourself and the following and then complete the sentence: "This intelligence product is about ...."

China: (This Intelligence Product Is About) Strides In Military Modernization

Your next challenge is make sure your topic sentence is tied to the title and contains an intelligence "so what."

* * *

When I first started out as a young intelligence analyst, I was amazed at the ability of the seasoned analysts to read vast amounts of source material on a given subject, and then conceptualize in one sentence the main analytic point from all they had read.

First, I had to realize there is no magic pill giving anyone the ability to pick out, much less conceptualize and articulate, the salient analytic point.

Second, I learned the ability to determine the main, overriding analytic point that needs to be made comes with experience and expertise.

Third, I also learned to trust my first impression, after I had gained on-the-job experience.

Let me give you an example of what I mean by point three. Below is an article on Hezbollah and Israel. The article is intelligence-rich. Please read it and underline the intelligence points.

Terrorism In Morocco

by Auroa Boringalis

The Virginia Mountaineer

Rabat, Morocco—In a major sting operation, the police in Rabat, in cooperation with Moroccan intelligence, arrested 35 suspected terrorists yesterday. Not only was the size of the operation a surprise, but the people arrested were not the run-of-the-mill terrorists. They were respected businessmen, government bureaucrats, a pharmacist, a police commander, and a TV journalist.

Authorities also seized a large arsenal of arms and ammunition. The profile of those arrested contrasts sharply with the profile of terrorists arrested six months ago. At that time police arrested several dozen young men from the slums of Casablanca. They had assembled homemade explosives and were preparing for a series of suicide bombings.

The latest arrests revealed a far more sophisticated terrorist operation. The leader of the group, Abdul al-Mani is a wealthy Moroccan immigrant in Belgium who is accused of financing his activity with multimillion dollar hold-ups and committing assassinations in that European country. He was arrested last week while he was on a visit from his home in Belgium where he lives with his wife and seven children.

Al-Mani is accused of committing half a dozen killings in Belgium since the late 1980s. The victims included a leader of the Belgium Jewish Community, the rector of a mosque, and a Syrian diplomat. The Belgian police were apparently not notified in advance of the charges and the arrest and were caught off-guard. Authorities in Brussels, however, have now opened their own investigation of al-Mani and the killings.

The Moroccan government has issued a statement saying that the 35-member group was plotting to assassinate cabinet ministers, military leaders, and prominent members of the Jewish Community.

The leaders of this group have trained in Afghanistan, met with al Qa'eda leaders and train regularly in rural Morocco. Some aspects of the case, however, puzzle terrorist specialists. For example, the three politicians arrested belong to small parties that mix Islamist and leftist ideologies. Their defenders describe them as moderates. But their longtime ties to Shiite Muslim movements, including Hezbollah, may have been a factor in their arrests. Sunni Muslims are in the majority in Morocco, but they worry about Shiite extremists.

"The group is a real mix of people and things, kind of bizarre, but if the charges against them are true, this is a big, big bust," said Claude Dubonnet, director of The Chablis Institute, a Brussels think tank. Dubonnet works for the Moroccan government as an adviser.

Morocco is relatively open and democratic, modernizing quickly and trying to reduce inequality. The monarchy promotes a tolerant Islam in which the king is leader of the faithful, an effort to maintain a bulwark against extremism. But its geography makes it a gateway to Europe and crossroads for migration, crime, and extremism.

On the east, Algeria has endured a campaign of suicide bombings by Al Qa'eda in the Islamic Maghreb, a network blamed for recent gun attacks to the south in Mauritania on French tourists and the Israeli Embassy.

Moroccan militants have gone abroad for training and combat. Some fight in Iraq and some trek to clandestine training camps in the deserts of southern Algeria and northern Mali. Intelligence experts say that there are several active channels to funnel fighters abroad. These militants also benefit from a boom in Europe-bound cocaine along traditional smuggling routes.

Moroccan authorities believe that some of those who were arrested played a role in planning and executing the 2004 Madrid train bombings. Most recently, the group appears to have been stockpiling

AK-47 assault rifles, Skorpio machine pistols, Uzi machine guns, and other weapons.

Moroccan officials believe they have crippled a major terrorist group. A group, officials speculate, that was planning widespread, large-scale attacks. A Moroccan intelligence officer, who declined to be identified by name, speculated, "We are dealing with the logic of a long-term, long-range terrorist group that had planned a strategy of infiltration in order to carry out their activities.

Now, look at the article again, and look at the parts I have underlined.

Terrorism In Morocco

by Auroa Boringalis

The Virginia Mountaineer

Rabat, Morocco—In a major sting operation, the police in Rabat, in cooperation with Moroccan intelligence, arrested 35 suspected terrorists yesterday. Not only was the size of the operation a surprise, but the people arrested were not the run-of-the-mill terrorists. They were respected businessmen, government bureaucrats, a pharmacist, a police commander, and a TV journalist.

Authorities also seized a large arsenal of arms and ammunition. The profile of those arrested contrasts sharply with the profile of terrorists arrested six months ago. At that time police arrested several dozen young men from the slums of Casablanca. They had assembled homemade explosives and were preparing for a series of suicide bombings.

The latest arrests revealed a far more sophisticated terrorist operation. The leader of the group, Abdul al-Mani is a wealthy Moroccan immigrant in Belgium who is accused of financing his activity with multimillion dollar hold-ups and committing assassinations in that European country. He was arrested last week while he was on a visit from his home in Belgium where he lives with his wife and seven children.

Al-Mani is accused of committing half a dozen killings in Belgium since the late 1980s. The victims included a leader of the Belgium Jewish Community, the rector of a mosque, and a Syrian diplomat. The Belgian police were apparently not notified in advance of the charges and the arrest and were caught off-guard. Authorities in Brussels, however, have now opened their own investigation of al-Mani and the killings.

<u>*The Moroccan government has issued a statement saying that the 35-member group was plotting to assassinate cabinet ministers, military leaders, and prominent members of the Jewish Community.*</u>

<u>*The leaders of this group have trained in Afghanistan, met with Al Qa'eda leaders and train regularly in rural Morocco.*</u> *Some aspects of the case, however, puzzle terrorist specialists. For example, the three politicians arrested belong to small parties that mix Islamist and leftist ideologies. Their defenders describe them as moderates. But their longtime ties to Shiite Muslim movements, including Hezbollah, may have been a factor in their arrests. Sunni Muslims are in the majority in Morocco, but they worry about Shiite extremists.*

"The group is a real mix of people and things, kind of bizarre, but if the charges against them are true, this is a big, big bust," said Claude Dubonnet, director of <u>The Chablis Institute</u>, a Brussels think tank. Dubonnet works for the Moroccan government as an adviser.

Morocco is relatively open and democratic, modernizing quickly and trying to reduce inequality. The monarchy promotes a tolerant Islam in which the king is leader of the faithful, an effort to maintain a bulwark against extremism. But its geography makes it a gateway to Europe and crossroads for migration, crime, and extremism.

To the east, Algeria has endured a campaign of suicide bombings by Al Qa'eda in the Islamic Maghreb, a network blamed for recent gun attacks to the south in Mauritania on French tourists and the

Israeli Embassy.

Moroccan militants have gone abroad for training and combat. Some fight in Iraq and some trek to clandestine training camps in the deserts of southern Algeria and northern Mali. Intelligence experts say that there are several active channels to funnel fighters abroad. These militants also benefit from a boom in Europe-bound cocaine along traditional smuggling routes.

Moroccan authorities believe that some of those who were arrested played a role in planning and executing the 2004 Madrid train bombings. Most recently, the group appears to have been stockpiling AK-47 assault rifles, Skorpio machine pistols, Uzi machine guns, and other weapons.

Moroccan officials believe they have crippled a major terrorist group. A group, officials speculate, that was planning widespread, large-scale attacks. A Moroccan intelligence officer, who declined to be identified by name, speculated, "We are dealing with the logic of a long-term, long-range terrorist group that had planned a strategy of infiltration in order to carry out their activities."

Now, craft a sentence that captures the main intelligence significance of the article. Once you have your sentence, look at three sentences done by students in my class. All three give the "what" and "so what," and all three could be the topic sentence for an intelligence paragraph or article.

As I said earlier, there is no magic pill an intelligence analyst can take to help him or her come up with the perfect topic sentence to capture the analytic significance of the whole piece. But, the Morocco article is an example of what I do. When I read raw intelligence for the first time, I underline my initial reaction, and nearly every time, the underlined sentences, phrases, and clauses are the core of the main intelligence assertion I make.

Terrorism In Morocco Sentences - Examples

1. Recent arrests in Morocco uncovered a well-established terrorist group whose members infiltrated into positions of trust.

2. The arrest of a large-scale white-collar terrorist network in Morocco may indicate al-Qa'eda's message has a broad appeal in emerging democracies.

3. The recent arrest of terrorists in Morocco reveals an evolution of terrorists' sophistication in identifying, targeting, and planning attacks on that country's leaders.

***

Next we'll discuss the problem we in intelligence analysts – analysts making wrong assumptions and then building their analysis on those assumptions.

Chapter 4

Assumptions

Assumptions are the siren songs of failed analysts' careers. A large number of intelligence failures can be traced back to intelligence analysts failing to challenge long-held assumptions, biases, or prejudices.

This book is not designed to teach methods for overcoming wrong assumptions, but it is meant to alert analysts to the seriousness of the problem by examining intelligence and crime scene failures stemming from wrong assumptions.

There are classes analysts can take to sensitize them to the problem of assumptions. These courses should be part of the curriculum of new analysts' training. There should be mandatory refresher courses on the problem of wrong assumptions for more experienced officers.

For the purpose of this book, let's take a look at an intelligence failure and a crime scene failure—both stemming from wrong assumptions. The first deals with the October War of 1973; the second with the shooting rampage at Virginia Tech.

The October 1973 War

On the morning of October 6, 1973, the CIA produced *The President's Daily Brief* carried an article asserting there would be no war in the Middle East. As that document was being delivered to the White House, Egyptian forces were crossing the Red Sea and establishing a beachhead on the Sinai Peninsula.

The nagging question is how could the CIA have been so wrong? Unfortunately, the answer lies, in large part, on wrong assumptions.

So, let's begin by looking at the factors leading up to October 6th that indicated war was imminent:

- Egyptian President Anwar Sadat had made public statements over the preceding three years that he was prepared to resort to war to get the Sinai back.

- In the spring of 1973, the Department of State's Intelligence and Research Bureau predicted there would be war.

- In September of 1973, there were extensive military maneuvers in Egypt and Syria involving the forward deployment of air defenses.

- On September 28th, Egypt cancelled all military leave.

- On October 4th, all Soviet dependents were evacuated from Egypt.

- The same day, October 4th, Egyptian civilian aircraft was grounded and the Cairo airport was closed.

- On October 5, 1973, Egyptian military forces deployed for offense action.

- Early in the morning of October 6th, a human asset, reading and seeing the above, broke his cover, went to a pay phone, and dialed a predetermined number to warn an attack was imminent.

- At 1400 on October 6, 1973, Egyptian forces crossed the Red Sea and the war began.

When you read the list of indicators above, you scratch your head and ask how could the CIA have been so wrong? The answer, in two words, is wrong assumptions. So let's take a look at the assumptions and indicators that specified there would be no war:

- The outcome of the six-day war in 1967, when Israel handily defeated Egypt, Syria, and Jordan in a three-front war, left the strong impression in the U.S., and the West in general, that Israel was almost invincible. Almost all policymakers thought it would be lunacy for Egypt to think it could go it alone militarily and defeat Israel.

- Throughout 1973, Egypt had conducted an unusually high number of military maneuvers—one on as large a scale as the September maneuvers— and there had been no war.

- Israel had mobilized in response to the large-scale Egyptian military maneuver in the spring of 1973, and there had been no war.

- Egypt was still pursuing negotiations to get the Sinai back through diplomacy, and conventional wisdom argued that as long as these negotiations were in progress there was no need for Cairo to resort to war.

- Egypt lacked air superiority. Again, conventional wisdom dictated no country would go to war when it knew from the outset it lacked air superiority.

- There was a general belief in Washington that the Soviet Union would not allow Egypt to go to war at a time when the U.S. and U.S.S.R. were engaged in détente— the initial thawing of the Cold War.

- U.S. policymakers were preoccupied with progress being made in Jordan's relations with Israel (and did not want to hear about a possible Egyptian- Israeli war unless there was iron-clad proof).

- There was no civilian preparation for war in Egypt. Usually there is a propaganda campaign to prepare the public for war—there was none at the time.

- The U.S. government asked the Israelis for their assessment of the prospects of war, and Tel Aviv responded the prospects were low.

- The Egyptian military mobilization/maneuvers in September were the 20th of the year.

- Egyptian and Syrian air forces were in defensive posture; there was no indication of preparation for an offense.

- On the night of October 5/6, when the CIA analyst tried to run an article in *The President's Daily Brief* saying war was imminent, the Agency checked with the Israeli embassy, who responded the chances of war were low. The article was withdrawn.

If you look at the lists above, you are struck by the fact the list of indicators of war is textbook perfect in predicting hostilities. Indeed, if you ever take a course in *Indications and Warnings*, you will see almost all those factors as reason to warn. On the other hand, the list of indicators of no war is almost all wrong assumptions, biases, and incorrect reading of the evidence.

Furthermore, the assumption in Washington was no country would go to war knowing it could not win on the battlefield. No one thought to look at other motivations for war such as the political incentive to get the talks moving toward returning the Sinai.

The assumption in Washington was that the U.S.S.R. would not allow Egypt to go to war. This was a complete misreading of the relationship between Moscow and Cairo and lack of understanding of the influence the Soviets had over Egyptian policymaking.

There was a belief (or assumption) that Egypt could not mount a large-scale, cross-water military offensive. But who was training the Egyptian military? The Russians. And how had the U.S.S.R. defeated Nazi Germany? By taking the offensive and forging one large river after another.

The assumption in Washington was Egypt would never go to war against Israel without the help of at least Syria (a two-front war).

Perhaps the most unforgiveable assumption of all was that Israel knew better than the evidence. In other words, we let our faith in Israel trump the evidence and our own Middle Eastern specialists' analysis of the situation. We let someone else do our thinking for us.

The fact Egypt carried out a masterful deception is not included in this list. As noted, Egypt had conducted 20 military maneuvers throughout the year. Those maneuvers involved advancing to the shore of the Red Sea. Each time the Egyptians returned to base, they left men and materiel in a forward position, conducting a highly successful, undetected, military buildup.

We also now know that when Egypt conducted large-scale maneuvers in the spring of 1973, it was prepared to go to war. Israel responded and mobilized. The bottom line is Cairo demonstrated it was capable of a highly sophisticated deception catching the mighty Israeli army off guard.

Finally, most policymaking and intelligence officials in Washington incorrectly assumed Egypt could never fool the Israelis when it came to matters and issues of war.

The Virginia Tech Rampage

The October 1973 war is a failure on the national level in the foreign affairs arena. The failure at Virginia Tech is on the part of the Virginia Tech Police Chief, the Cook Counseling Center, and the school's president and governing body—the Policy Group.

In the case of Tech, in order to understand the magnitude of the catastrophe that sprang from wrong assumptions, you have to remember there were two shooting incidents on the morning of April 16, 2007. The first was at 7:15 a.m. when two students, Emily Hilscher and Ryan Clark, were murdered in West Ambler Johnston dormitory. And, the second was between 9:40 a.m. and 9:51 a.m. in Norris Hall where 30 students and faculty members were massacred, and 17 others were wounded.

The assumptions in question are those made at the time of the double homicide. Indeed, those wrong assumptions played a role in the deaths of 30 people and the wounding of 17 others. Those same wrong assumptions were then glossed over in the intelligence report/analysis commissioned by then-Governor Tim Kaine. So, let's take a look at what happened on that morning:

- Virginia Tech Police Chief Wendell Flinchum, who was in charge of the investigation, decided that because there was a dead male student in his underwear and a dying female student in her pajamas, and that this was a "domestic incident." In other words, some sort of love triangle.

- Virginia Tech Police Chief Wendell Flinchum incorrectly assumed, because this was a "domestic incident," the killer was off the campus and would not return. He was wrong on both accounts.

- Virginia Tech Police Chief Wendell Flinchum built on his incorrect initial assumptions, and made another wrong supposition that it was not necessary to warn or lockdown the campus.

- Virginia Tech Police Chief Wendell Flinchum learned an hour into the investigation that Emily Hilscher had a boyfriend who owned a gun and liked to target practice. This fact solidified his initial assumptions to the exclusion of all other possibilities. The Virginia Tech police named Emily's boyfriend, Karl Thornhill, a person of interest. In concentrating on Thornhill, Flinchum downplayed the possibility someone else might be the murderer, and he or she might be a threat to the campus.

- A far more likely explanation of the crime scene was that Ryan Clark, the Resident Assistant whose room was next to Emily's, heard Emily's call for help, and did not take time to put his pants on before going to investigate. Furthermore, it was well known Clark was gay. A domestic incident or love triangle, along the lines Chief Flinchum was thinking, was out of the question. A questioning of students in the rooms near Hilscher and Clark would have debunked all of Flinchum's incorrect assumptions.

* * *

Assumptions then can make or break intelligence analysis. In talking with an instructor at the FBI Academy in Quantico, Virginia, she volunteered one of the common mistakes analysts make is they don't recognize embedded assumptions made in the initial Intelligence Question. For example, how will a country change its modus operandi in the United States after an Intelligence Officer was PNGed back to country X?

The assumption is country X will change its modus operandi. The question should be will country X change the way it does business in the wake of one of its officials being PNGed, and if so, how? There is a good possibility country X will not change its modus operandi.

In the final analysis, Intelligence Analysts have to remember assumptions can be logical and rational, but they can be wrong. They must challenge their assumptions all the time.

Chapter 5

Short Products

Some of the most important written intelligence products are one paragraph or less. During my career at the CIA it was fairly common for me to produce a one-sentence intelligence item for one of the Agency's daily publications. One sentence may not be exactly the right terminology, because these items consisted of three parts separated by ellipses.

Here is an example:

> *Romanian Prime Minister Bobelescu arrives in Paris today…talks with Premier Devereaux start tomorrow … increased bilateral security cooperation main topic.*

Many times I have work all day on a daily full-page intelligence report for *The President's Daily Brief,* only to have management reduce it to a one-line item.

If a longer piece of intelligence is going to be reduced to a one-sentence item, the editor will turn to your topic sentence. So, here again you see the importance of conceptualization, knowing the main intelligence point you want to make and capturing it in the topic sentence.

The need to be brief and concise cannot be overstated when it comes to intelligence writing. We are not academics; we are a cross between journalists and academics. Remember, the President's day is planned in five-minute intervals. We have to combine the journalist's skill of presenting information in a tight format with the academic's emphasis on thoroughness and accuracy.

The journalist tries to get the "who, what, when, where, and why" in the first sentence; the intelligence analyst tries to get the bottom line up front (BLUF) or the "what and so what (sometimes the what next)" in the topic sentence. We cannot play fast and free with facts and evidence, nor can an analyst allow his or her bias or prejudice to influence the selection of those facts and evidence.

If the President or primary consumer of your intelligence wants to know more, she or he will ask.

Writing Is Thinking On Paper

Now is a good time to remind you that writing is thinking on paper. One of the reasons why many people dislike writing is they know intuitively that they are saying many things about themselves when they put pen to paper, or fingers to keyboard. You are telling people, rightly or wrongly, your level of education, your knowledge of English, your ability to use English correctly, and your thought processes. For Intelligence Analysts the later point is especially important. If your writing is unclear and muddled, the reader will conclude your thoughts and logic are muddled. Your intelligence will not be read.

You are telling the reader your level of education by how you present your argument, your vocabulary, and your use of grammar. If your writing is sloppy English, the reader gets a sloppy impression of the author. If your writing is filled with spelling and grammar errors you tell the reader you didn't care enough about what you had to say to proof read.

Any writing that is well done requires a considerable amount of thought before the author puts pen to paper or fingers to keyboard. Sound intelligence writing requires that the author knows the main point he or she wants to make, and puts point up front.

As underscored in Chapter 3, a vital part of good writing is conceptualization. Thinking and conceptualizing about what you will write are key elements to producing a clear and concise draft. If you know what you want to say ahead of time, then the drafting is easier.

Once you know what your thesis is, then you can to put your ideas on paper. Writing for the workplace is plain talk, straightforward and matter-of-fact communication. You must be committed to simplicity of expression, precise wording and determination to reveal what you mean.

Clear And Logical Thinking

The success of your intelligence analysis will probably rise or fall on the logic of your argument. Therefore, check and double-check your facts to be certain of their accuracy. Avoid the temptation to ignore facts that run counter to your argument— you may even want to explain why you disagree. By addressing facts that run counter to your thesis, you add credibility and objectivity. Remember, you want to be as objective as possible, especially when you are asking the reader to accept your interpretations. The following are some points to keep in mind as you write:

- Use accurate and verified data. Facts and evidence are the basis of judgments. The truthfulness and accuracy of your evidence is paramount to convincing the reader of your argument.

- Use reliable sources. When citing written works, use the most recent and reliable possible. If using open source material, try to use only the best authorities in the field and make that the language and tone of the work are reasonable.

- Avoid sweeping generalizations. Generalizations are at best imperfect and there are so many exceptions to generalizations that they can be counter-productive to your thesis.

- When crafting your topic sentence you need to rise to a level of generality that captures the main point of your whole argument, but is not so broad as to be meaningless.

- Do not clutter your text with too many statistics. Statistics and samplings of opinions, as well as polls and other kinds of data are important to proving your argument. But, use them carefully and think about separating them from the text and putting them in charts, graphs, or text boxes. Stick to the point. Remember the argument you are trying to make—discard interesting but irrelevant material.

- Do not ignore conflicting facts or evidence. Be aware of facts and evidence that refute your argument—deal with them fully and honestly.

- Avoid asking questions. If you ask the reader to answer a question, you may not get the response you want. Furthermore, intelligence analysts' main job is to answer questions, not raise them.

Analysts' and Reviewers' Checklist

Below is a handy-dandy checklist for analysts to use before they turn in their drafts to management. It is not perfect, but it is a good place to start.

- The draft has the main point in the first sentence; I call it the bottom line up front (BLUF) or the "what" and "so what." Some intelligence writing instructors call it "the statement of synthesis," "the big picture, bottom line," or the strong topic sentence."

- The draft is analytical (uses words like assess, judge, believe, estimate, think, anticipate) at the beginning of the paper and tells the reader the what, the so what/analytical judgment (why the bottom line message is important and relevant), and the implications or consequences of the assessment.

- Words indicating probability are used (remote, unlikely, likely, probably, certain, estimate, think, or anticipate) to show analysis and to indicate the likelihood of events occurring or to come.

- Source summary statement, descriptors, and citations—as appropriate.

- The main points contain the major judgments (key arguments) supporting the bottom-line assessment of the document.

- All main points are clearly supported by evidence differentiating between what you know, what you assume, what you presume, what you think, and what you don't know (intelligence gaps).

- All information in the intelligence product relates directly to the bottom line.

- The body of document supports the message in a logical order apparent to the reader.

- The draft contains no inconsistencies or contradictions in conclusions and information; if alternative analysis (as appropriate) is presented, confidence in the alternatives should be indicated and be consistent with the document as a whole.

- The draft presents information in a prioritized fashion (for example, page 2 is less important than page 1; page 3 is less important than page 2).

- If the draft ends with a summary (only longer intelligence products), no new information is presented that is not included in the initial paragraph.

- Graphs are used to add meaning to the document and are easy to understand.

- The draft is straightforward, concise, and precise.

- Language used in the draft is correct (active voice, active verbs, lack of extraneous qualifiers, and there is parallelism in components of the sentences).

- The mechanical aspects of the draft are correct (grammar, spelling, punctuation).

- The draft does not contain unnecessary passive voice sentences.

- You have used the correct verb tense. A common error is for analysts to use present tense when they mean past tense.

- The vocabulary is clear and concise; the words are readily understood on the first reading so that the reader does not have to go to the dictionary.

- Be careful of spell-check, it only tells you that you have spelled an English word correctly, not if you have used the correct English word. If you mean to write too, but write two, spell check will not pick up the error.

- Remember, the grammar and punctuation function in Word is only about 47% accurate. The figure goes down when it comes to intelligence writing because we do not conform to standard academic or American English. Sometimes we are conforming to legal English.

My definition of a short intelligence article is between one and two paragraphs—a page at the very most. So let's look at the basic paragraph again.

The title of your intelligence product is the contract with the reader and then you deliver on that contract in the topic sentence. Remember, if you can go to the last sentence of your paragraph and can say, "Most importantly dear reader, don't forget" you have failed the Inverted Pyramid intelligence style of writing.

The next category of short intelligence products is the two-paragraph products.

Two Paragraph Intelligence Separating Analysis From Facts

Title – Contract With The Reader

Ideally, it should be between four to six words. The formula for the title is: Use the country name or subject matter such as Terrorism followed by a colon. Then in four words tell the reader briefly what the intelligence report is about. This is your contract with the reader. For example:

Egypt: Attempted Assassination of President

First Paragraph - The Topic Sentence

The topic sentence delivers on the contract. This sentence contains the main analytic judgment. This paragraph contains evidence and facts. The analysis is developed further in the second paragraph. For example:

Egypt: Attempted Assassination of President

President Anwar Sadat was wounded today during a military parade, but a coup does no appear to be in progress.

First Paragraph

The rest of the first paragraph develops the topic sentence, and further delivers on the contract. By advancing the analytic judgment. This paragraph expands and develops the analysis.

President Anwar Sadat was wounded today during a military parade, but a coup does not appear to be in progress, according to the U.S. embassy in Ronu. No official medical bulletin has been released. Vice President Mosseq, also wounded in the attack, is meeting with the cabinet. Ronu, according to the embassy, is calm and troops are concentrated around government installations. Three U.S. military personnel were injured in the attack.

Title (Contract with the reader) → Deliver on the Contract

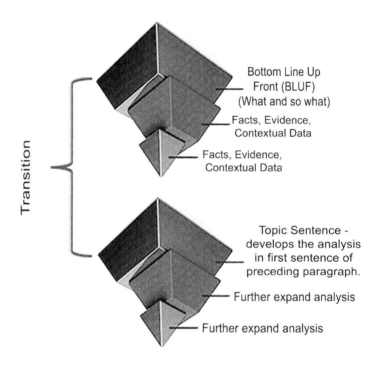

Type Script Memorandum Format

I am using the typescript memorandum format to illustrate a multi-paragraph piece of intelligence.

Executive Summary

The typescript memo almost always begins with an Executive Summary. The topic sentence of the Executive Summary contains the main analytic judgment of the whole memo. In addition it contains four or five sentences of secondary judgments, facts, and possibly an outlook statement.

Paragraphs 2-5

These paragraphs advance or substantiate the analysis. The second paragraph may contain some sort of historical perspective limited to no more than three sentences.

Paragraph 6

This paragraph is the last paragraph in the multi paragraph analysis. The last paragraph frequently some sort of forward thrust, or what the reader can expect. In other words, you are telling the reader "what next".

The key to using the Inverted Pyramid Paragraph structure is to put your main analytic point (the "what" and "so-what") in the first topic sentence. Then, put the main analytic point (the "what" and "so-what") for each subsequent paragraph in the topic sentence of that paragraph.

You also need to remember that in a traditional paragraph you know you are done because you tell the reader the main point. In the Inverted Pyramid paragraph, the main point comes first and you know you done, when you the analyst, are have presented the best evidence to support the analytic thrust you are making.

Now, on to longer papers.

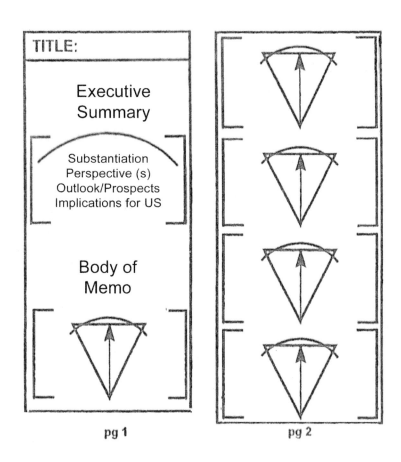

pg 1   pg 2

Chapter 6

Longer Products

Before you begin to work on any intelligence product you need to ask yourself some questions and have it clear in your mind what the paper is intended to do and what intelligence question(s) it answers.

Frequently, longer papers (I mean two or more pages) are the result of a customer request. But often those requesting your analysis are not clear; you are not sure what you are being asked to address or what question(s) the requester wants answered. So, you need to define what is being asked by giving the request considerable thought. The simple answer is to go back to the requester to get more specific. Unfortunately that rarely happens, so the analyst is left on her or his own to determine the thrust of the paper.

In the 1990s we used to run an exercise at CIA training designed to assist future analysts define vague requests. Here it is:

> *Congressperson "x" has asked the CIA to write a short memorandum explaining what will happen once Mainland China takes control of Hong Kong.*

The question is not clear. The analyst therefore has to give his or her response careful thought. First, the analyst needs to determine what are the intelligence questions surrounding this problem. Here are some possibilities:

1. Will Beijing throw out Hong Kong's capitalist economic system and superimpose a state-owned, centrally controlled communist economy and thereby run the danger of losing the former British colony's economic clout in the Far East?

2. Will Hong Kong's financial enterprises and economic resources flee Hong Kong in fear that they will be nationalized?

3. If Hong Kong's economic enterprises decide to relocate to other areas of the Pacific Rim, in what cities or countries are they likely to relocate?

4. If Beijing superimposes a communist political system on Hong Kong, doing away with the ex- colony's more democratic, representational government, will there be political and social unrest?

The question is probably best restated as, "What are the political and economic ramifications of Hong Kong's returning to Chinese control?" The memorandum can then go into subsections answering the following questions:

- Will China keep Hong Kong's capitalism, modify it, or superimpose a communist economic system?

- Will Hong Kong's financial institutions relocate to another city along the Pacific Rim? If so, which city or cities?

- How will China deal with Hong Kong's democratic system of government?

- How will China deal with citizens' rights such as freedom of speech and freedom of assembly?

Once you have defined the problem and decided what the intelligence question is, then you can begin to work. I would suggest you use the following checklist from the outset of your work and refer to it throughout your research and writing.

Check List For Planning Your Project

The Audience

Who is the principal consumer? This question is not as easy as it looks. The principal consumer may not be one person; it may be a group of people. For example you may write for policymakers, you might decide to write in order to float your analysis for your fellow analysts' consideration. Here, you need to know the groups of consumers who receive the publications for which you write.

- What issues are the customers' grappling with or concerned about?

- What function should or will the paper serve? Inform? Forecast? Alert?

The Intelligence Question

- What is the key intelligence question the paper will address?

- What is the most important message the paper will convey?

Scope Note—How The Analyst Plans To Bound The Issue/Paper

I will go into Scope Notes in Chapter 7. I have to confess that I never used a Scope Note during my career as an Intelligence Analyst. Scope Notes were just beginning to be used at the end of my career. I have, however, become a big fan of them and as you will see in Chapter 7, I used a Scope Note in writing my book on the Virginia Tech shooting. Briefly, here are the bare bones of what you should be thinking about when drafting a Scope Notes:

What does the analyst need to consider as he or she develops the key message or main analytic point? Consider addressing levels of confidence in judgments and sources, key sources used, critical gaps in knowledge, methodologies (if any), and what the paper will and will not cover. You may also want to include the timeframe:

This paper covers the period of August 2014 to April 2015.

You probably also will want to tell the reader what the paper does not cover, and why.

Thesis Statement And Structure

As you have read over and over again in this book and my other writings, take time to conceptualize a working thesis statement— or your "what" and "so what" and possibly the "why." This thesis statement can, and probably will, adjust and modify as you do your research.

Once you are well along in your research, take time to draft a working outline, and if possible, notional subtitles. In longer papers, these notional subheadings will greatly aid the reader in moving through your paper. The subheadings also help clarify and organize the information for you, the drafter, about where you should place facts and data. Sometimes evidence can and does support a number of different points you are making. You do not want to repeat yourself, so the subheads can help you decide where the evidence best fits.

Let's take a closer look at subtitles. After your title and the initial topic sentence, subtitles may be the most important part of a longer paper.

Subtitles

The subtitles should have an analytic thrust and tell the reader what they can expect the section to address. Subtitles are an invaluable aid to readers when looking at longer papers. They help keep the reader focused as he or she transitions from one section to another. Subtitles help tighten the organization and focus of an analytic product. In brief, subtitles:

- Highlight key analytic points.

- Convey the main point or content of each section.

- Link sections of the paper together.

- Combine with the title to relate the bottom line of the whole paper.

- Help keep similar things together.

- Group information by main points, themes, topics.

- Can be arranged along a timeline to tell a story.

Points supervisors can suggest analysts consider when drafting subtitles include:

- Write analytic subheadings for each main point/theme/

topic rather than use words such as "background" and "conclusion."

- Give careful thought to the arrangement of subheadings, possibly in a timeline to tell the story. Or, arrange subtitles in descending order of importance.

Supervisors should encourage all analysts to write analytic subheadings for longer papers. Encourage analysts to write analytic subheadings for each main point/theme/topic. In many cases subheadings are arranged along a timeline to tell the story.

Subtitles, then, help keep like things together; they group information by main assertions, themes, and topics; they play an invaluable role by helping readers follow the logic and analytic message of the paper.

Graphics

I cannot stress enough the importance of good graphics. Facts and evidence are vital parts of an intelligence product, but they can sometimes weigh down and interrupt the flow of the narrative. Good graphics can take these facts and evidence, remove them from the narrative and put them in a quickly understood and visually digestible form for the reader.

If your product is rich in evidence, facts, and statistics, think not only of graphics in the text, but appendices to support your assertions. Appendices give the reader the option of whether or not to read the details. Appendices also, just as with graphics, help the flow of your intelligence narrative by removing details. I once wrote a long intelligence report that was four pages of narrative and 12 pages of appendices.

Use maps, graphs, charts, photos, or any graph to buttress the message you are trying to convey. Give considerable thought to what kind of graphic will enhance your product; what detail and information can be removed from the text and put in a graphic. I particularly like using text boxes for background, timelines, photographs, and charts. The saying, "A picture is worth a thousand words," is true.

Structuring An Analytic Product

An analytic product usually moves forward from what is happening now and what it appears to mean, to what will probably happening next. Another way to put it is an analytic product moves from what is known or you think you know, to what is unknown.

The current or the "what" (what is happening now) should make it clear to the reader why he or she should spend his or her valuable time reading your product. It includes what you know, what is happening or has happened, it may include the "why." The current often includes the how you know—in other words, the source.

The future, or the "so what," should include the significance or main analytic point you are making. The "what" and "so what" may also be followed by subsections dealing with:

- Long-range outlook

- Broader implications

- Opportunities for the U.S. or your intelligence organization to exploit. (I will examine Opportunity Analysis in more detail in Chapter 11.)

Gaps in knowledge are also an important part of longer intelligence products. A section dealing with gaps does two things, first, it tells the reader why you could not address certain aspects of the subject you are addressing, and second, it helps guide collection.

Other key ingredients of an analytic paper:

- The title, which is your contract with the reader. You deliver on the contract in the thesis or topic sentence. Readers often decide whether or not to read a paper based on the title.

- Analytic subtitles can be invaluable in helping hold the paper together and advance the analytic argument.

- Topic sentences for each of the subtitled sections should capture the main point of what follows.

Chapter 7

Scope Notes
A Tool For Managers
And Analysts

Scope Notes were just being introduced as standard practice at the CIA when I moved from producing intelligence to training intelligence analysts. So I cannot say that I ever used them on the job. My first thought when I heard about Scope Notes was they were just another bureaucratic hurdle we need to jump over to get our longer products out. I was wrong. Scope Notes are an excellent way of establishing a contract between the analyst and his or her supervisor.

Scope Notes

Scope Notes are an excellent tool for analysts and managers. Once I learned more about them, I quickly became a big fan of Scope Notes.

For the analyst, Scope Notes can save a lot of time and work. More than once, I have discussed a project with a supervisor and gone away thinking we were in sync on the thrust of the paper only to find out when I submitted the outline that we were miles apart.

Some intelligence products also publish a Scope Note at the beginning of a paper. This is an excellent use of a Scope Note because it helps the reader understand what is in the following papers and why.

Now let's take a look at the seven main ingredients of a Scope Note. You do not have to include all seven, but if you can it will greatly aid reviewers and readers.

* * *

Just to review, the purpose of the Scope Note is:

- To help supervisors and analysts have a clear, common understanding of the objectives, and a definition of what the paper will and will not cover.

- To allow the analyst to articulate the analytic framework of a paper.

- To aid the reader's understanding what the paper is about, will cover, and (equally important) what it will not cover (and why).

The following are the seven topics that are addressed in Scope Notes. Again, there may not be a need to address them all; however, addressing as many of them as possible can you save you major headaches down the road. Here are the seven:

1. Analytic Framework:

- Describe what key intelligence issue is being addressed in the product.

- Provide a time frame for the paper. For example, this paper covers the period from January 2012 to December 2014.

- Give the reader a warning that certain aspects of the subject will not be covered in the paper that he or she might expect. You may or may not want to tell them the reason for the exclusion(s).

2. Comment On Previous Production

- Tell the reader if this is the first time the subject has been addressed. Implicit in this is the fact that the paper meets the thresh hold of his or her interests and thus deserve to be read.

- Let the reader know if the paper revisits a core analytic line, thesis, or intelligence problem, the reader should be made aware of the fact.

- Alert the reader to the fact the paper is part of an ongoing analysis. You can also mention other related papers.

3. Key Assumptions

- Tell reader the key assumptions that underpin the analysis.

- Alert the reader to more complex or controversial intelligence questions addressed in the paper. You need to articulate the underpinnings of the reasoning in and for the paper.

- Repeat the assumptions mentioned in the body of the paper, to remind the reader of them.

4. Sourcing

- Explain the type and variety of sources used to produce the intelligence paper. You do not have to be specific; general categories such as open, humint, or comint are acceptable.

- Highlight heavy dependence on a particular type or source of reporting. Types or sources of reporting give insight into the reliability of the report. For example, if the report relies heavily on press reporting, the reliability is more questionable.

- Mention a unique source that gave you insight into the topic (clandestine source, case studies, academic methodologies, etc.).

- Mention any official travel you used to gather information.

5. Analytic Tools Or Methods

- Alert the reader to any analytic tools, approaches, techniques, or methodologies used.

- Provide any unique insights these techniques or capabilities brought to the analysis.

- Define methodologies if unfamiliar to the customer. This is often listed at the bottom of the Scope Note, and the text is italicized.

6. Contacts and Collaboration

- Mention if paper draws on input from academics or outside consultants, and what they brought to the table.

- Give credit to other Intelligence Community agencies that collaborated or coordinated on your product.

- Note any different views from your own (if they are significant), and explain why you discarded them.

7. Definitions

- Provide definitions of terms used in the assessment if those terms are not well known or their meaning can be misinterpreted.

- Consider directing readers to a glossary of terms at the end of the paper, if there are too many terms that need definition to put in the Scope Note. (Also consider defining key terms in text boxes throughout the paper).

* * *

Now that we have discussed Scope Notes, their importance, and what goes in them, let's take a look at some examples.

The following are examples of Scope Notes:

Scope Note #1

This paper assesses the threat of Chinese military intelligence collection inside Canada, with special emphasis on Canadian high- tech companies and government entities involved in foreign policy. The information for this report was obtained from a highly reliable source as well as from several intercepts. The intercepts cover the period from early November, 2011 to mid-January, 2012. This assessment does not include other potential threats from Chinese clandestine operations, nor does it deal with specific Canadian counterintelligence efforts.

Scope Note #2

This report examines the dangers of cyberterrorism and cyber attacks that may be tried against U.S. nuclear facilities. It examines scenarios under which extremists would use cyberterrorism to attack the United States and why. It does not go into the capabilities of various extremists groups such as al-Qa'eda to do so in the near future. Sources for this report were primarily derived from open press and the television network al Jazerra. The author also met with scientists in the U.S. nuclear program, as well as counter-terrorism experts throughout the U.S. policy and intelligence communities. The author met with leading academics in the field of nuclear security.

* * *

These Scope Notes are examples based on traditional intelligence topics. When I was working on my book about the Virginia Tech shooting, I decided to write a Scope Note in connection with that program—a true crime exposé and analysis.

If any of you enjoy writing and do some creative writing on the side, I would suggest you think about a Scope Note, if for no other reason that they help you stay focused. They can also be part of a package you send in a proposal to a publisher, and can (and often should) be published with the book. The Virginia Tech Scope Note is on the following page:

Virginia Tech:
Make Sure It Doesn't Get Out

(The Virginia Tech Tragedy from the Victims' Perspective)

This book examines the missed opportunities, in the wake of the Virginia Tech shootings on April 16, 2007, to do something significant to improve campus security and to help prevent future school shootings. The author discusses his reasons and motives for writing, the problems the victims' families have faced and continue to face in their efforts to find the truth, as well as the misconceptions about what took place before, during and after the Tech massacre. The book contains a detailed analysis of the Governor's Review Panel Report and will look at what parents can do to help ensure the safety of their children on our campuses. This book deals with those who exploited the shootings for their own ideological and personal reasons. The author draws on over 50 years of work in intelligence and crime analysis, over 14 years of research and writing on school shootings in Virginia, numerous scholarly works on school safety, personal interviews with victims and their families, and a plethora of news accounts and reactions to the shootings at Virginia Tech. Finally, the author bring to the book his personal experience in having lost a family member in a Virginia school shooting.

Enough of Scope Notes. I think you get the idea, and see their importance. Next, it is time to turn our attention to three areas about which there is some confusion: *Bullets, Key Judgments,* and *Executive Summaries.*

Chapter 8

Bullets, Key Judgments, And Executive Summaries

We have examined sentences, paragraph, and both short and long papers. I would be remiss if I did not address three aspects of intelligence writing that all members of the community share in common: *Bullets*, *Key Judgments*, and *Executive Summaries*. There is some, not a lot, but some confusion about them, and I will try to clear that up. I will begin with Bullets.

Bullets

The Intelligence Community loves Bullets because they break out facts, evidence, and complicated information and put them in a visually digestible format. Bullets are frequently a phrase, clause, or a sentence or two. Unlike Key Judgments and Executive Summaries they can and do appear anywhere in the text of an intelligence project. As I said, they are extremely helpful in breaking complicated thoughts and ideas into their discrete sections and presenting them so they can be read and understood quickly. For example, in presenting a series of statistics or facts that are related, Bullets hold the reader's attention. If you put those same statistics or facts in a long sentence, the reader's eyes will glaze over. Indeed, to put those same facts or statistics in a narrative would require a compound-complex (or run-on) sentence. The reader will not bother wading through such a sentence. However, the reader will be drawn to Bullets because they are easy to read and send the signal that the author has taken time to arrange important facts, statistics, or evidence into a format that is easily read. *Bullets* also can be used for emphasis.

The following is an excellent example of Bullet use from one of my students. The exercise is to read a 30 plus-page Case Study on the collapse of U.S. policy toward Lebanon and the Middle East in the early 1980s. The students read the case study and then, in no more than 125 words, had to tell me what lessons they took away from the Study. One student chose to use Bullets to emphasize the three main lessons he took away from the Case Study.

Lebanon Case Study

The Reagan Administration's ill-fated Lebanon policy was doomed to failure because of a failure of communication between the Intelligence Community and policymakers. The Intelligence Community's inability to successfully communicate concerns— combined with policymakers disregard for intelligence— contributed to the deaths of 241 Americans. The following points are the main lessons for intelligence analysts:

- *Do not allow accepted practices to prevent your analytical judgments from being voiced. Regarding Lebanon, analysts shied away from commenting on policy, despite well-founded misgivings.*

- *Do not assume your message is conveyed unless you explicitly state it. Cautionary information about Lebanon in PDBs and NIDs failed to get the message to policymakers in the absence of a comprehensive Estimate.*

- *Do not let institutional barriers prevent you from conducting analysis or disseminating critical information.*

Executive Summaries And Key Judgments

Executive Summaries and Key judgments are among the most important parts of an Intelligence Analysts' writing, because both are often the only section of the intelligence product that key consumers read. I led this chapter with Bullets because they are frequently part of both Executive Summaries and Key Judgments. Indeed, Bullets often are basic building blocs of both Key Judgments and Executive Summaries.

Executive Summaries

Executive Summaries appear at the beginning of many longer intelligence products. They are often just labeled Summary. Whether you call them an Executive Summary or Summary, they are essentially the same thing and contain the main analytic points contained in the body of the report or memorandum that follows.

The importance of Executive Summaries cannot be overstated because often primary consumers only read summaries. Remember, intelligence analysts are vying for people's time. Most senior decision makers will not take time to read even a two-page document. They want their intelligence in one paragraph of no more than six or seven sentences. If we peak their interest, they will read the whole product. In the meantime, an assistant to the decision maker should read the entire report and be ready to answer questions from his or her boss. Intelligence analysts are often writing for two audiences—the primary consumer and the assistant.

On the following page is an example of a fictitious memorandum prepared for a high-level U.S. policymaker who is preparing to make a fact-finding trip to Somewhereistan. The policymaker wants to be brought up to date on the current situation, and has asked for a briefing memorandum on Somewhereistan. For the purposes of this exercise we will call the memorandum a Situation Report.

Somewhereistan:Situation Report
Executive Summary

Somewhereistan appears to be on the brink of major ethnic violence between the Uhrue minority and the Ebod majority that could undercut government stability, pose a threat to the President's rule, and eventually undermine U.S. interests in the region. Internal control is deteriorating and the country's Internal Security Minister is responding with actions that will further incite, rather than calm, tensions. The violence has divided the government between the hardline policies advocated by the Internal Minister and the more accommodating approach toward the ethnic minority, (the Uhrues) being pursued by the President. Relations between Somewhereistan and its neighbors, particularly Northistan, are strained because of the ethnic tension. Northistan is predominantly Uhrue. The President will probably ask for U.S. assistance, both economic and military, but will stop short of offering the U.S. a military presence on Somewhereistan soil. Any increased U.S. military presence in the region could alarm Somewhereistan's neighbors, most of whom would probably view a U.S. military presence as an intervention in the region's affairs.

This *Executive Summary* tells the senior U.S. official the gist of what he or she needs to know, and provides a blueprint for what the official can expect to find in the body of the memorandum. Indeed, that is one of the cardinal features of an *Executive Summary*; it gives the substance of the critical analytic judgments and tells the reader approximately what order they will be addressed. In this case, the *Executive Summary* alerts the decision maker to serious ethnic strife, a sharp division within the government, and what the Somewhereistan President will probably seek from the U.S. The details, facts, and evidence are in the body of the memorandum.

A cardinal rule of both *Executive Summaries* and *Key Judgments* is never introduce anything in them that is not in the body of the main report.

Key Judgments

Key Judgments are used for longer intelligence papers. There is no one set style for *Key Judgments* other than they should, as the title suggests, contain the key judgments and conclusions of the intelligence product. *Key Judgments* are almost always longer and more detailed than *Executive Summaries*, and contain supporting evidence, something not normally included in *Executive Summaries*. Stylistically, *Key Judgments* combine both *Bullets* and paragraphs, and they sometimes will include graphics. The most notable use of *Key Judgments* is in Estimates, but they are by no means limited to that product. They appear in many assessments, reports, and memoranda.

On the following page are the *Key Judgments* from the unclassified *November 2007 National Intelligence Estimate, Iran: Nuclear Intentions and Capabilities*. The *Key Judgments* are an excellent example of combining different styles of presentation in a premier intelligence product.

National Intelligence Estimate
November 2007
Iran: Nuclear Intentions And Capabilities

Key Judgments

A.

We judge with high confidence that in fall of 2003, Tehran halted its nuclear weapons program*. We also assess with moderate-to-high confidence that Tehran at a minimum is keeping open the options to develop nuclear weapons. We judge with high confidence that the halt, and Tehran's announcement of its decision to suspend its declared uranium enrichment program and sign an Additional Protocol to its Nuclear Non-Proliferation Treaty Safeguards Agreement, was directed primarily in response to increasing international scrutiny and pressure resulting from exposure of Iran's previously undeclared nuclear work.

We assess with high confidence that until fall 2003, Iranian military entities were working under government direction to develop nuclear weapons.

We judge with high confidence that the halt lasted at least several years. (Because of intelligence gaps discussed elsewhere in this Estimate, however, DOE and the NIC assess with only moderate confidence that the halt to those activities represents a halt to Iran's entire nuclear weapons program.)

We assess with moderate confidence Tehran had not restarted its nuclear weapons program as of mid-2007, but we do not know whether it currently intends to develop nuclear weapons.

We continue to assess with moderate-to-high confidence that Iran does not currently have a nuclear weapon.

Tehran's decision to halt its nuclear weapons program suggests it is less determined to develop nuclear weapons that we have been judging since 2005. Our assessment that the program probably was halted primarily in response to international pressure suggests Iran may be more vulnerable to influence on the issue than we had judged previously.

B.

We continue to assess with low confidence that Iran probably has imported at least some weapons-usable fissile material, but still judge with moderate-to-high confidence it has not obtained enough for a nuclear weapon. We cannot rule out that Iran has acquired from abroad—or will acquire in the future—a nuclear weapon or enough fissile material for a weapon. Barring such acquisitions, if Iran wants to have nuclear weapons it would need to produce sufficient amounts of fissile material indigenously—which we judge with high confidence it has not yet done.

C.

We assess centrifuge enrichment is how Iran probably could first produce enough fissile material for a weapon, if it decides to do so. Iran resumed its declared centrifuge enrichment activities in January 2006, despite the continued halt in the nuclear weapons program. Iran made significant progress in 2007 installing centrifuges at Natanz, but we judge with moderate confidence it still faces significant technical problems operating them.

We judge with moderate confidence that the earliest possible date Iran would be technically capable of producing enough HEU for a weapon is late 2009, but that is very unlikely.

We judge with moderate confidence Iran probably would be technically capable of producing enough HEU for a weapon sometime during the 2010-2015 time frame. (INR judges Iran is unlikely to achieve this capability before 2013 because of foreseeable technical and programmatic problems.) All agencies recognize the possibility that this capability may not be attained until after 2013.

D.

Iranian entities are continuing to develop a range of technical capabilities that could be applied to producing nuclear weapons, if a decision is made to do so. For example, Iran's civilian uranium enrichment program is continuing. We also assess with high confidence that since fall of 2003, Iran has been conducting research and development projects with commercial and conventional military applications—some of which would also be of limited use for nuclear weapons.

E.

We do not have sufficient intelligence to judge confidently whether Tehran is willing to maintain the halt of its nuclear weapons program indefinitely while it weighs its options, or whether it will or already has set specific deadlines or criteria that will prompt it to restart the program.

Our assessment that Iran halted the program in 2003 primarily in response to international pressure indicates Tehran's decisions are guided by a cost-benefit approach rather than a rush to a weapon irrespective of the political, economic, and military costs. This, in turn, suggests that some combination of threats of intensified international scrutiny and pressures, along with opportunities for Iran to achieve its security, prestige, and goals for regional influence in other ways, might—if perceived by Iran's leaders as credible— prompt Tehran to extend the current halt to its nuclear weapons program. It is difficult to specify what such a combination might be.

We assess with moderate confidence that convincing the Iranian leadership to forgo the eventual development of nuclear weapons will be difficult given the linkage many within the leadership probably see between nuclear weapons development and Iran's key national security and foreign policy objectives, and given Iran's considerable effort from at least the late 1980s to 2003 to develop such weapons. In our judgment, only an Iranian political decision to abandon a nuclear weapons objective would plausibly keep Iran from eventually producing nuclear weapons—and such a decision is inherently reversible.

F.

We assess with moderate confidence that Iran probably would use covert facilities—rather than its declared nuclear sites—for the production of highly enriched uranium for a weapon. A growing amount of intelligence indicates Iran was engaged in covert uranium conversion and uranium enrichment activity, but we judge that these efforts probably were halted in response to the fall of the 2003 halt, and that these efforts probably had not been restarted through at least mid-2007.

G.

We judge with high confidence that Iran will not be technically capable of producing and reprocessing enough plutonium for a weapon before about 2015.

H.

We judge with high confidence that Iran has the scientific, technical and industrial capacity eventually to produce nuclear weapons if it decides to do so.

***

Key Differences between the *Key Judgments* of this *Estimate* on Iran's Nuclear Program and the May 2005 Assessment are presented in the table on the following pages.

* For the purposes of this Estimate, by nuclear weapons program we mean weapon design and weaponization work and covert uranium conversion-related and uranium enrichment- related work; we do not mean Iran's declared civil work related to uranium conversion and enrichment. program.

2005 IC ESTIMATE	2007 NATIONAL INTELLIGENCE ESTIMATE
Asses with high confidence that Iran currently is determined to develop nuclear weapons despite its international obligations and international pressure, but we do not assess that Iran is immovable.	Judge with high confidence that in fall 2003, Tehran halted its nuclear weapons program. Judge with high confidence that the halt lasted at least several years. (DOE and the NIC have moderate confidence that the halt to those activities represents a halt to Iran's entire nuclear weapons program.) Assess with moderate confidence Tehran had not restarted its nuclear weapons program as of mid-2007, but we do not know whether it currently intends to develop nuclear weapons. Judge with high confidence that the halt was directed primarily in response to increasing international scrutiny and pressure resulting from exposure of Iran's previously undeclared nuclear work. Assess with moderate-to-high confidence that Tehran at a minimum is keeping open the option to develop nuclear weapons.

2005 IC ESTIMATE	2007 NATIONAL INTELLIGENCE ESTIMATE
We have moderate confidence in projecting when Iran is likely to make a nuclear weapon; we assess that it is unlikely before early-to-mid next decade.	We judge with moderate confidence that the earliest possible date Iran would be technically capable of producing enough highly enriched uranium (HEU) for a weapon is late 2009, but that this is very unlikely. We judge with moderate confidence Iran probably would be technically capable of producing enough HEU for a weapon sometime during the 2010-2015 time frame. (INR judges that Iran is unlikely to achieve this capability before 2013 because of foreseeable technical and programmatic problems.)
Iran could produce enough fissile material for a weapon by the end of this decade if it were to make more rapid and successful progress than we have seen to date.	We judge with moderate confidence that the earliest possible date Iran would be technically capable of producing enough highly enriched uranium (HEU) for a weapon is late 2009, but that this is very unlikely.

Next we look at editing. All intelligence analysts (all writers) should welcome good editing. I believe that there is something that stands between the author and the ability to produce an error- free written product. That something rests on the fact that analysts (authors) are bogged down in detail. We know what we want to say, so we miss errors in logic, argumentation, and presentation. An editor can spot and fix those problems; an editor can take a solid first draft and turn it into an outstanding product.

Chapter 9

Editing

I believe there is something that stands between the author and the ability to put a draft in succinct, well-written publishable format. Yes, there are a few people who can do this, and I have worked with some. But for the rest of us mere mortals, we need help. We need an editor to bridge this gap. The mark of a good writer is one who seeks out and welcomes editing. In my opinion, a good editor is worth his or her weight in gold.

There are many stages to writing. Editing begins when you put pen to paper or fingers to keyboard because you're sorting your thoughts and organizing as you write. You will probably go through many drafts before you submit your work to a supervisor, reviewer, or editor.

A good rule of thumb is there are four stages to editing and the first stage is editing done by the author. This editing begins the first time the intelligence officer begins to put her or his thoughts on paper. This stage is most often called brainstorming. At this point don't worry about spelling, sentence structure, grammar, or punctuation— just get the ideas out. You begin to edit as you go over your thoughts and look for patterns or clusters of thoughts.

The second stage is where you begin both the analysis and writing. You look at your ideas and begin to group them together. You also begin the first stage of serious self-editing. In order to start this process you must edit to make sure you have English sentences— specifically, intelligence sentences telling what your analysis means. You are both analyzing and editing at this stage— the two cannot be separated.

The third stage is a multi-step analyzing and editing process. Now you look at your draft to make sure you have answered all the questions related to your analysis. You review and edit for the organization and logic of your argument. You should edit for sentence structure, spelling, grammar, and punctuation. Finally, you look at your work for style and professionalism—have you presented the best intelligence possible? At this point, all that has gone into getting you this far—your creativity and analysis— stands in the way of producing the final, professional piece of intelligence. And so, now comes the critical last state.

The fourth, and perhaps most important stage, is when you give it up. You give your draft to someone else to read. This is the stage that most of us think about when we think of editing. A good editor can take a solid, well written intelligence draft and turn it into an outstanding intelligence product. But, there is much more at stake at this stage. The editor or reviewer must give the intelligence analyst clear editorial feedback if the analyst is to avoid making the same mistakes and develop into a good intelligence writer. It is not acceptable to tell a drafter, "This is not what I want. I don't know what I want; do it over again. I'll know it when I see it."

What follows are some rules that can help both the analyst and editor in reviewing and revising papers.

Rules For Editing

The following are 10 easy rules to remember that will help you with editing:

1) Edit for simple, readable sentences. A simple easy-to-read sentence avoids rambling ideas and multiple clauses. Simple sentences are easy for the eye to digest.

2) Keep the average sentence length to 15-17 words.

3) Keep one main idea to a sentence.

4) If the sentence is too long (25 words or more), try to break it into two or more sentences.

5) Periodically throw in a sentence of five or six words—or less.

6) Use a conjunction or connective (and or but) to start a sentence.

7) Occasionally, long sentences are fine. Just double check to make sure they are clear, punctuated correctly, and can be read once and understood.

8) Use proper word order. For example, make sure modifiers are in the correct place.

9) Make sure the message conveyed is the one that is intended.

10) Keep related parts of the sentence together.

Five Reviewing /Editing Principles

If you are editing or reviewing someone else's paper there are some simple principles to follow. Indeed, most intelligence professionals say there are five most important editing and reviewing principles for intelligence writing:

1. Apply standard intelligence writing principles to your feedback. For example.

    - Strong topic sentences that capture the "what" and "so what." This sentence may be referred to as the bottom line up front (BLUF) "statement of synthesis," or the "big picture, bottom line."

    - Use the Inverted Pyramid Paragraph structure, if the template calls for it. If not, be able to explain the logic and organization of the paragraph.

    - Point out areas where the accepted Intelligence English is not Standard American English.

2. Do Not Rewrite The Paper.

    - Give the author examples of how the argument should be made and the correct sentences and words that she or he should use.

3. Tell the author where he or she can find the justification for the editorial changes.

    - For example: Your organization's style guide. Many members of the Intelligence Community use *The Gregg Reference Manual*.

4. Be Specific.

    - If possible differentiate between the mandatory style and the editor's personal preference.

5. Do not say, "This is not what I want. Do it over again. I will know it when I see it."

Checklist

The following is a checklist for both analysts and reviewers when going over drafts.

✓✓   The draft has the main point in the first sentence (the Bottom Line Up Front (BLUF)).

✓✓   The draft is analytical (uses words like assess, judge, believe, estimate, think, anticipate) at the beginning of the paper and tells the reader the <u>what</u>, the <u>so what/analytical judgment </u>(why the bottom line message is important and relevant), and the <u>implications or consequences </u>of the assessment for the United States and/or your intelligence organization.

✓✓   Words indicating probability are used (remote, unlikely, likely, probably, certain, estimate, think, or anticipate) to show analysis and to indicate the likelihood of events occurring or to come.

✓✓   Source summary statements, descriptors, and citations are used as appropriate.

✓✓   The main points contain the major judgments (key arguments) supporting the bottom line assessment of the draft. If the reader takes nothing else away from the intelligence document, it will be this point and it is in the first sentence---the BLUF.

✓✓   All main points are clearly supported by evidence differentiating between <u>what we know, what we assume, what we think, and what we don't know </u>(intelligence gaps). Some intelligence organizations now require a section on intelligence gaps in all their major studies.

✓✓   All information in the draft relates directly to the bottom line.

✓✓   The body of the draft supports the message in a logical order, and that order is readily apparent to the reader.

✓✓   The draft contains no inconsistencies or contradictions in conclusions and information; if alternative analysis (as appropriate) is presented, confidence in the alternatives should be indicated and be consistent with the document as a whole.

✓✓   The draft presents information in a prioritized fashion (for example, page 2 is less important than page 1; page 3 is less important than page 2).

✓✓   If the draft begins with a summary (only longer intelligence products), no new information is presented in the summary that is not included in the body of the paper.

✓✓   Graphics are used to add meaning to the document and are easy to understand.

✓✓   The draft is straightforward, concise, and precise.

✓✓   Clarity and language used in the draft are correct: active voice, active verbs, lack of extraneous qualifiers, and there is parallelism in components of the sentences.

✓✓   The mechanical aspects of the draft are correct (grammar, spelling, punctuation, use of numbers, acronyms, etc.)

You Say Tomatos And I Say Tomatoes

There are a number of pitfalls in English that trip up the best of writers and introduce errors into otherwise well-done drafts. For example, I can never remember whether or not to put an "e" on the end of a word ending in "o" before making it plural. I almost always have to look them up. Here a few of the those words with their plurals:

Singular	Plural
tomato	tomatoes
potato	potatoes
patio	patios
torpedo	torpedoes
hero	heroes
cameo	cameos
domino	dominoes
piano	pianos
echo	echoes
radio	radios
video	videos.

Who Or Whom?

The words "who" and "whom" confuse almost everyone, unless you have a degree in English. A good way to remember the difference is this, "who" is in the nominative case, where a nominative pronoun can be used. If you can substitute the words "I," "we," "he," "she," "you," or "they," then "who" is correct. "Whom" is in the objective case. If you can substitute "me," "us," "him," "her," or "them" use "whom."

For example, it is incorrect to say, "Who did you bring to the party?" You should say, "Whom did you bring to the party?" You are the subject of the sentence and "who" needs to be "whom" in the objective case.

Do You Email Or E-Mail?

For some reason, some managers in government, and private business have decided that when it comes *"email"* or *"e-mail,"* the hyphenated version is correct and ensuring that everyone uses the hyphen is a personal crusade. In fact, both are correct, but "email" is the preferred standard. The bottom line is that both are correct.

If for no other reason than your personal knowledge, here is the reasoning for making "email" the preferred choice. The preference comes from the words *ebusiness, ebooks,* and *ecommerce* evolved have evolved over time, *email* therefore should follow this model.

So You Have A Degree

The question of whether or not to capitalize a person's academic credentials can cause confusion. So remember, the words "bachelor," "master," and "doctor" are capitalized when following a person's name (Sally Smithenheimer, Doctor of Divinity). They should be lowercased with an apostrophe in the following: I have a master's degree. I am enrolled in a master's program in education.

Are You Blatant Or Flagrant— Or Neither?

Two words that are frequently used incorrectly are "blatant" and "flagrant." Remember them this way, "blatant" means offensively loud, conspicuous, or obtrusive. "Flagrant" means glaringly offensive or deplorable; scandalous. True, we all know people whose personalities combine both words— hence the confusion.

For example, "Donald Trump engages in blatant verbal retaliation against his critics." On the other hand, "Donald Trump's threat to ban all Muslim immigrants from the U.S. is a flagrant violation of the principles of non-discrimination."

We Tend To Per Incorrectly

I have trouble remember when and how I should use "per" and "as per." The fact is you should not use them. Instead, in professional writing use "as," "according to," (in some instances, although I don't think it sounds professional) "as usual," or "in response to."

For example you should not begin a response with "per you letter of January 20th…." Instead, write "In response to your letter of January 20th.

An Iffy Problem

The use of "if" is always a problem. The reason "if" is a problem is there are times when you write or say, "If I were…." and there are times when you write or say, "If I was…….."

One way to remember which construction is correct is to think of the problem this way—use "if I were…" when what you are talking about is contrary to fact. For example: "If I were king, I would give everyone a palace."

Use "if I was…" when the statement may be true. For example: "If I was rude, I am sorry." The fact is you were rude, so "was" is the correct form.

This May Or Might Interest You

Then there is the problem of the difference between "might" and "may". One way to think about it is that "might" is a weaker form of "may." Something that "might" happen is less a possibility than "may" happen.

The dictionary tells you that "might": is the past tense of "may." So, you would write, "She might have broken her leg." In the present tense it is correct to use both: "She may break a leg," or "She might break a leg."

"Might" is also the past tense of "may." You would use might when referring to the past. For example, if you intended to go to the gym last night, you would not say, "I may have gone to the gym last night, but instead I ate a pizza." Instead, you would say, "I might have gone to the gym last night, but instead I ate a pizza."

The second example is a gray area. When writing about something that may not occur, it is better to use might as the reader may assume you are referring to permission. For example, "We may not go to the gym," can be misinterpreted to mean you do not have permission to go to the gym, particularly in writing where voice inflection do not help the recipient follow your meaning. If you say, "We might not go to the gym," you meaning is clear.

Use may when the outcome is likely and might when the outcome is less likely or uncertain. Use might when writing about negative outcomes, even if the outcomes are likely, and if using may would make people think you were talking about having permission.

Keep An Eye On The Verbs

Verbs are an essential part of English sentences and in Intelligence writing they are critical to the point the analyst is making.

The importance of the verb begins with selection. Verbs carry the power of the message the analyst is making. You want to select just the right verb; it should not be too weak and undercut the message you are conveying, nor should it be too strong and over state the point of your analysis.

Pay close attention to verb tenses. When I was in school the rule was writers should not change tenses in an English sentence. If a writer wanted to change tenses in a sentence, he or she was supposed to stop and start a new sentence. The rule now says it is correct to change tenses in professional writing in an English sentence. The problem is that we Americans probably have the shortest attention span of any people on the face of this earth. The new rule says "It is correct to change tenses in a English sentence ..." (at this point many Americans stop paying attention and fail to read the rest of the rule) "...if you have a reason." You must have a reason to change tenses.

What has crept into our language (even in professional writing), as a result of the relaxation of this rule, is many people, in both speaking and writing, are defaulting to the present tense when they really mean past tense (or on occasion future tense).

Tenses are also important because of the expectations they arouse in the reader's mind. If your intelligence is in the past tense, the implications are probably going to be more definitive and clearly defined. If your intelligence is in the present tense or continuous present tense, then the implications are probably going to be more open ended, and perhaps more speculative. If you use the future tense, then your analysis may be very speculative and often include alternatives.

Before we leave the subject tenses. It is a good idea to remind ourselves of the fact that English has verbs in transition from older forms of the past tense. For example, there are few verbs where it is correct to have a past tense ending with "ed" or with "t." For example, both of the following are correct:

✓✓ He spilled the milk.

✓✓ He spilt the milk.

✓✓ She burned the toast.

✓✓ She burnt the toast.

Here are more verbs that can use either the "ed" or "t" to form the past tense. (The most common or preferred usage is listed first.)

✓✓ bereaved (bereft)

✓✓ dreamed (dreamt)

✓✓ knelt (kneeled)

✓✓ learned (learnt)

✓✓ leapt (leaped)

✓✓ leaned (leant)

✓✓ spelled (spelt)

✓✓ spoiled (spoilt)

Taking the "ed" or "t" issue a step further, here is an idiosyncrasy of the past tense involving some verb forms ending in *t* or *d* have dropped "ed" endings in the past tense. For example, we once said: "Mr. Jones 'betted' on the wrong horse and lost all his money." "His suit 'fitted' well." "She 'wedded' her high school sweetheart." Now we say, "Mr. Jones 'bet' on the wrong horse and lost all his money." "His suit 'fit' him well." "She 'wed' her high school sweetheart."

To Be Or Not To Be

Then there is the verb "to be," which can pose some interesting problems.

There are times when you use the "be" form of the verb "to be" rather than "was" or "were." Use "be" when someone *suggests, demands, asks, requests, requires,* or *insists.* For example:

✓✓ The judge ordered that he be executed.

✓✓ I demanded that I be allowed to attend.

✓✓ I was asked if I would be there.

✓✓ The law requires that you be in court.

Subject-Verb Agreement (A Quick Reminder)

I know you know this, but I am going to remind you anyway. Make sure you have subject-verb agreement. If you have a singular subject, then you need a singular verb.

A few years ago I was asked to teach for a major intelligence organization. When I got there, to say that the atmosphere was tense does not begin to describe what I found. The person sponsoring the class told me the reason for my presence. The intelligence unit had produced a finished product and taken it to their director.

The director read the first sentence, stood up, and threw it across the room. He then told them, "If I get one more product from you with subject-verb disagreement, I will fire all of you. I will get analysts who know this basic principle of English."

That is a bit of an over reaction. Yes, the principle is simple, but it is an easy mistake to make because in English we are encouraged to move the subject around in a sentence in order to add to the style and keep the readers' interest. Just remember, if you have a "single subject" you need a "single verb;" a "plural subject" takes a "plural verb."

Recently I saw a piece of law enforcement intelligence that had the mistake: "New York is one of the few states that have gun laws." New York is the subject, so the verb form must be the singular "has." The author had obviously made the verb "have" agree with the preceding plural noun "states."

A Final Word: Conceptualization

You are probably tired of hearing me make this point, but it deservers to be repeated. When you edit or a review a paper make sure that *the main point*, the *statement of synthesis*, *the big picture-bottom line*, *the* BLUF (bottom line up front) or the *what and so what* is the lead. That way if the reader takes nothing else away from the intelligence product, he or she will know the main point you want to make.

Taking the time to conceptualize the main analytic point will not make the writing easy, but it will make it so much easier. And remember, make sure your title is the contract with the reader and you deliver on that contract in the all- important first sentence.

Next, let's move to a problem all intelligence analysts face— deception. Is the opposition trying to mislead you, hid intentions, lull you into making wrong analyses? The answer is "yes."

Chapter 10

Deception Analysis

Deception, in its many forms, is an every day problem intelligence and crime analysts face. From self-deception, in the form of biases and prejudices, to the deceptions carried out by the opposition, deception is omnipresent and deserves attention in this textbook. Indeed, I would advise all intelligence officers to take a course in denial and deception early in their careers.

Most texts on deception concentrate on deception as carried out in a military or political context, failing to recognize self- deception is a major cause of intelligence failures. A friend of mine, with over 40 years experience in intelligence, tells his classes that no analyst can come to a problem or situation with a clean slate. He or she will always have preconceptions or assumptions. The assumptions may be correct, but the analyst fails to step back and reevaluate them when dealing with a new problem. Judgments, he says, tend to get firmer in the analysts minds and they rarely revisit them.

Sometimes self-deception and deceptive practices of the opposition come together and result in devastating consequences.

The October 1973 War

The October 1973 War is a case in point. Egypt carried out a masterful military deception as it built up men and materiel on the shores of the Red Sea. The most insidious parts of this deception were perceptions and assumptions by Washington and Tel Aviv that blinded U.S. and Israeli intelligence officers and policymakers to what was going on under their noses. The assumptions and biases include Israel is invincible; no country would start a war knowing it could not win on the battlefield (failing to take into account there may be other reasons for starting a war such as to get the talks revitalized to return the Sinai Peninsula to Egypt); or Egypt would not start a single front war, it would, at minimum, need Syria to open a second front. And many in Washington believed that the Soviet Union would not permit Egypt to start a war—a total misreading of the relationship between Cairo and Moscow, not to mention an exaggeration of the control Moscow had over any non-bloc state with whom it had close relations.

In the final analysis, it was the self-deceptions mentioned above that ensured there would be a major U.S. intelligence failure. On the morning of October 6, 1973, the *President's Daily Brief* carried a lead article stating there would be no war in the Middle East. Within hours of the President reading this, Egypt crossed the Red Sea and the war began. It is hard to ignore an intelligence failure of that magnitude.

To show the power of self-deception's ability to neutralize facts and evidence, let's examine the indicators Egypt would go to war versus Egypt would not go to war. The lists of indicators of war and no war are just a broad look at the events of 1973. The lists are intended to give you an idea of how assumptions undercut the evidence. The lists are by no means all-inclusive.

Indications War Would Break Out

- Egyptian President Anwar Sadat had repeatedly said he was prepared to go to war to get the Sinai Peninsula back.

- State Department's Intelligence and Research Bureau (INR) warned in the spring of 1973 that Egypt was getting ready to go to war to regain the Sinai.

- Egypt began large-scale, extensive military maneuvers in September 1973.

- Egypt's September military maneuvers involved the forward deployment of air defenses.

- On September 28, 1973, all Egyptian military leave was cancelled.

- The USSR launched an extra reconnaissance satellite on October aimed at the Red Sea and Sinai Peninsula. (The Soviet Union was Egypt's principle military trainer and supplier.)

- On October 4, 1973, NSA warned that hostilities are imminent.

- The Soviet Union evacuated all dependents from Egypt on October 4, 1973.

- All Egyptian civilian aircraft were grounded and the airports at Cairo and Alexandria were closed October 4th.

- Egyptian forces were deployed for offensive action on October 5th.

- A source in Egypt went to a pay phone and broke his cover; he called a predetermined emergency, number to warn Egypt is ready to strike. That was at 0400 on October 6th.

- Egypt launches an attack on the Sinai at 1400 on October 6th, established and held a beachhead on the peninsula.

Indications War Would *Not* Break Out

- The outcome of the six-day war in 1967 had made Washington believe Israel was nearly invincible—and certainly would be able to repel any invader. Egypt starting a war it knew it could not win on the battlefield was beyond the comprehension of most intelligence officers and policymakers.

- Egypt had conducted numerous maneuvers throughout 1973 and there had been no war. All of the maneuvers involved men and materiel moving to the Red Sea. The maneuvers were a masterful deception because every time the troops withdrew they left some of the men and equipment on the shores of the Red Sea. There were a total of 20 Egyptian military maneuvers throughout 1973 until war broke out in October.

- Israel had mobilized in May 1973 in response to similar large-scale Egyptian military maneuvers and there had been no attack. Mobilizations are expensive and disrupt the Israel economy. (We now know that Egypt would have attacked in May had Israeli not mobilized. In early October 1973, Tel Aviv was reluctant to repeat an expensive mobilization without conclusive evidence the threat was real.)

- Egypt lacked air superiority and conventional wisdom dictated that no country goes to war without air superiority.

- Egypt was pursuing negotiations to get the Sinai back, and Washington assumed that no country would go to war when it stood a chance of getting what it wanted through negotiations. There was a belief in Washington that Moscow would not allow Cairo to start a war.

- There was a belief in Washington that Moscow would not allow Cairo to start a war.

- U.S. policymakers were preoccupied with relations between Jordan and Israel and did not want to be told war between Egypt and Israeli was likely.

- There was no civilian preparation for war in Egypt.

- Syrian forces were in a defensive posture after an air battle with Israel.

- The Egyptian air force was in defensive posture until the last minute. U.S. policymakers assumed Egypt would not attack Israel without a second front—Syria.

- Israeli military intelligence, when asked by U.S. officials, assessed the risk of war as low. (The U.S. Government and the CIA let someone else do their thinking.)

- On the morning of October 6, 1973, the lead CIA article in the *President's Daily Brief*, estimated the possibility of war between Egypt and Israeli as low.

- The October 1973 War may be one of the most stunning examples of bias, assumptions, beliefs, and wishful thinking converging with a masterful military deception to catch the enemy (Israel) and its chief ally (the U.S.) flat footed. These need to conform with the list of indications of war.

* * *

I covered biases and assumptions at length in Chapter 4, but wanted to briefly return to the subject to remind readers that our own assumptions and biases (as well as those of others) are a form of deception.

One way to check assumptions/biases/preconceptions is to set back and say to yourself, "What am I not seeing that I should be seeing if my analysis is correct?"

Now on to the more traditional look at deception—what the

opposition does to try and fool us. The next chapter draws heavily on notes taken at a U.S. government-sponsored conference on deception in the 1980's. It is not the author's original work.

Chapter 11

The Possibility Of Deception

(Note: The material in this chapter is based on a
US government conference on deception.)

The possibility of deception must always be on the minds of intelligence analysts. Deception can be a significant factor in complex intelligence issues that hampers our efforts to reach confident conclusions. This is true whether we are analyzing a particular political issue or attempting to determine whether a human source is under the control of a foreign intelligence service.

The word deception carries baggage. No one cares to admit that one's analytical judgment has been flawed by undetected deception—being deceived suggests we are naïve or have not devoted sufficient time and energy to the problem.

Deceptions, in their many forms, are as old as the history of mankind itself—the Trojan horse being one of the most famous. Deception and deception analysis came to the fore in the eyes of the U.S. public during World War II. One of the most famous deceptions is the Allies' elaborate creation of a phony invasion army in northern England under the command of General George Patton. The deception was aimed at Hitler and his generals and intended to convince them that the Allied invasion of Europe would be at Calais. The ruse was so successful that Hitler was convinced and beefed up German defenses far from the Normandy landing site.

During the Cold War, some Western politicians saw Soviet and Communist deceptions everywhere. They saw Soviet machinations and deception everywhere, all aimed at undermining NATO and Western democracies. It is hard to measure how accurate their fears were, but there is no doubt that Moscow did engage in elaborate deceptions. The Soviets had two broad categories of deception:

Active Measures (Aktivnyye Meropriyatiya): referred to a broad range of activities designed to achieve short-and long-range objectives by shaping opinion in the targeted country. Active measures actions were approved at the highest levels of government and coordinated with overt policy initiatives, such as propaganda and diplomacy. Active measures essentially were part of a form of perceptions management.

Maskirovka referred to military deception operations or actions designed to mislead an enemy about the strength, disposition, objectives, combat readiness, and other military capabilities of one's own forces. The Soviets had extensive literature on *Maskirovka*. Techniques including cover, concealment, false radio signals, dummies, decoys, and planted articles (disinformation in military journals to mislead and confuse). In military maneuvers or actual warfare, feints in one area suggesting strength and action, while concealing main force positions and actual strike intentions in another area, are an example of *Maskirovka*.

In the U.S. Intelligence Community there are basically two schools of thought on deception in the intelligence world. The first is a broad definition referring to: political or military strategy that conceals its true goals; propaganda, active measures, policy statements by the national leadership that implement strategy; concealment or misrepresentation of information to gain an advantage during negotiations of any kind; and measures to limit knowledge of strategy weapons, installations, or activities. This definition of deception is all encompassing, covering military, political, economic, and social activities; it is the one most people use.

The second, broader definition of deception is: An action or set of coordinated actions intended to mislead through the creation or perpetuation of false perceptions with the objective to induce the opponent to act, or react, in a way prejudicial to his or her interests. More simply: To have an adversary act in a way not in his best interest, but without the adversary realizing what is being done and, more importantly, who is doing it.

This second approach to deception defines the word more narrowly, using it to refer to only a limited set of activities. Advocates of this definition make distinctions between broad perception management activities aimed at policymakers and the public, and disinformation passed through controlled intelligence channels (double agents or compromised technical collection systems) for the purpose of deceiving the opposition. This activity is aimed at deceiving intelligence analysts. According to intelligence sources, advocates of the narrower definition argue that only this latter activity is properly termed deception. Some in the second camp also draw a sharp distinction between deception and such activities as camouflage, cover, and denial.

Deception then has numerous meanings, all of which are legitimate in the context within they are used.

I vote for the broadest possible definition of deception. As indicated earlier, I would go for a much more extensive, all inclusive interpretation of deception because I believe self- deception is, in many respects, the most insidious form of deception and it affects all of us.

Approaching Deception From Different Angles.

Others approach deception from different angles. Here again are two other ways to define the word—involving two broad categories of deception: perception management (a sophisticated form of intelligence aimed at the public and decision makers) and intelligence deception (aimed at intelligence organizations). The short definitions for the two are:

Perception Management	refers to activity and actions directed to or at policymakers, decision makers (including intelligence analysts), and the public. The channels used are deceptive or false statements by prominent individuals, politicians, leaders, and others including arms control negotiators, covert placement of articles in newspapers, forgeries, agents of influence, and propaganda through front organizations or groups, visitor exchanges, and the media.
Intelligence Deception	is deception directed specifically at intelligence services through controlled human sources or technical intelligence channels.

According to many U.S. intelligence agents, the analytical importance of this distinction cannot be overstated. Perception management, practiced by the former Soviet Union in peacetime, was pervasive; confirmed instances of intelligence deception, however, were the exception rather than the norm. In wartime, in contrast, intelligence deception would likely be far more common.

For perception management, impact is of paramount importance. What is its impact on U.S. policymakers? Does the deception influence U.S. intelligence analysts or U.S. intelligence products? The big question is, can or should U.S. intelligence, or some element of the government, play a more active role in combating the impact of perceptions management on foreign governments, U.S. policymakers, or U.S. public opinion?

Having said the above, there are a number of subcategories of deception with their own specific definitions. Let's take a moment and look at a list of those categories and their definitions.

The list of terms included is neither inclusive nor an "official" U.S. Intelligence Community definition of terms. The list is, however, based on deception analysis training done throughout the U.S. Intelligence Community.

Denial:

Denial includes routine operational security, such as practiced by military forces; it also includes withholding information deemed sensitive at the time. Denial, strictly speaking, is not deception; but denial activities are usually a part of any major deception operation. Generally, denial measures are intended to promote uncertainties in assessments, whereas deception is intended to lead an opponent toward erroneous conclusions. The terms "passive" and "active" provide guidance in differentiating between denial and deception.

Disinformation:

The dissemination of false, half-true, or misleading information—often combined with truthful information— is designed to achieve a certain objective. Disinformation is similar to propaganda with the following differences:

Propaganda is aimed at a mass audience, either domestic or foreign, and is not necessarily deceptive; disinformation, in contrast, is aimed only at a specific foreign targets, is purposely deceptive, and is part of a covert intelligence operation.

Perceptions Management:

The manipulation of perceptions concerning aims and policies directed primarily at key audiences— policymakers, the media, business, scientific, and academic elites, and the public. Channels used include statements by political leaders, articles placed in newspapers and journals, and use of a variety of other overt and covert measures to achieve the particular objective.

Strategic Deception:

A strategic deception is a major deception program designed to achieve a major national objective. Such a program involves multiple deception plans and an array of deceptive techniques. Examples: the deception operations carried out by the Allies preceding, (and continuing afterwards), the Normandy landings in 1944 that misled the Germans into thinking that Calais was the major landing area; and the Trust organization in the 1920s whereby the USSR lured most of the anti- Soviet émigré organizations to return to the Soviet Union.

"The Concept Of Lying" Encompasses That Of "Cover."

Liars not only hold back truth; they also act to deflect their victims away from it, thus highlighting deception's positive side. Liars create and perpetuate falsities and seek to draw their victims' attention to them.

Deception And Lying Are Not Exactly Synonyms:

Lying looks primarily to one side of the interaction between liars and their audience. Lying stresses the actions of the tellers of falsehoods. *Deception* is a term of wider scope because it also stresses the reactions of the receivers of falsehoods.

Eventually almost all deceptions are exposed as events unfold; thus the trick for the deceivers is to ensure that their lies are accepted long enough to benefit them.

The immediate aim of deception is to condition a target's beliefs; the immediate aim is influence his or her actions; and the ultimate aim is for the deceiver to benefit from the target's actions.

There are two variants of deception as defined by those who practice deceiving.

The first is "ambiguity producing" Type A: Here deceivers act to confuse their targets by confronting them with a least two choices as to what the truth may be. ... The greater the number of compelling alternatives, the smaller the possibility that the targets may, by chance, settle on the true one as the basis for action.

The second is more complicated and is labeled "misleading" or Type M deceptions: There are at least three types of this deception:

- The M-1 type deception attempts to have the victims accept as true that which they are already inclined to believe.
- The M-2 type deception is the most difficult because the deceivers swim against the tide of the victims' predispositions. The goal is to have the victim believe something he or she is inclined not to believe.
- The M-3 type deception concerns those cases in which the victims' predispositions (prior to the commencement of the deception) are not directly relevant to or predictive of what the victims come to accept as the truth.

Finally, it is worth noting that for intelligence deception, the key questions concern both existence and impact. For example, is deception of technical intelligence collection systems limited to camouflage, cover, and denial, or is there active manipulation of information fed through these systems? If limited to camouflage, cover, and denial, does it nevertheless bias the intelligence product? Is intelligence deception limited to tactical and operational level, or is it guided by some grand strategic design?

* * *

As you can see by the material in this chapter, deception is an umbrella concept that has several meanings and includes many different forms of activity. Objective analysis and accurate communications will be helped to the extent that we avoid the general term deception and refer instead to the more specific form of activity that falls under this general heading.

I hope I have sensitized you to the problem; peaked your interest; and stimulated you into taking courses on the subject.

Chapter 12

OpportunityAnalysis

The term Opportunity Analysis has been around a long time. Historically it has been use by economists to define marketing opportunities, including looking at the current state of an industry, company, or market in order to determine where there is room to attract more customers, introduce new products, sell products or achieve company growth.

Opportunity Analysis is the Intelligence Community's answer to making intelligence useful and actionable for policymakers. The question of how close intelligence analysts should come to policymakers has led to spirited debates. The subject has been hotly debated, and in some quarters still is.

Initially the Intelligence Community erred on the side of more academic, scholarly studies, which shielded them from having to draft actionable (or opportunity) intelligence.

Opportunity Analysis involves analyzing the opposition or a target and making recommendations on weakness that U.S. policymakers can exploit to their interests. Opportunity Analysis usually centers on long-range strategic objectives.

Tactical Intelligence is usually more immediate and more perceptive. Tactical Intelligence is frequently urged by the military in planning battles, or my police intelligence in order to assist a police operation.

History Of Opportunity Analysis

I date CIA's use of *Opportunity Analysis* to Bob Gates' time as Deputy Chief of Intelligence. There always had been something called "vulnerability analysis," but it was mainly tied to specific intelligence operations, rather than broader strategic analysis and long-term goals. But before Gates' tenure was over, *Opportunity Analysis* would become a part of the CIA's arsenal of analytic products.

Gates, in the early 1980s, had served a rotational tour to the National Security Council where he made a strong, positive impression. Indeed, that impression was so strong that Gates, who had left CIA a Soviet analyst, returned as one of the Agency's most powerful leaders, the Deputy Director for Intelligence.

The NSC had repeatedly criticized CIA intelligence products for being removed from policymaker needs, the intelligence was well written and interesting but was not actionable; it had little or no practical use from the policymaker's perspective. Analysts had to be taught that Opportunity Analysis is about what could be done, not what should be done. Intelligence analysts also need to be reminded that input into any foreign policy decision anywhere in the world is the same, how will it play in domestic politics? The job of the analyst then, is to identify the actions (or inactions) that could influence things and leave it up to the decision makers whether they want to pay the price.

Gates set out to provide his former colleagues at the Executive Office Building with analyses providing insights going beyond traditional intelligence products by identifying opportunities to advance U.S. policies. *Opportunity Analysis*, as Gates saw it, could also provide insights into ways to counter or mitigate threats to the U.S. or allied interests.

Gates also envisioned *Opportunity Analysis* identifying levers that can be exploited to advance U.S. interests and have a positive affect on outcomes. Opportunity Analysis is not policy prescriptive.

Examples:

1. How the U.S. might adapt its approach vis-à- vis the Taliban to take advantage of Afghan sentiments for peace.

2. How can the FBI or police departments leverage increased gang violence to improve reporting from angered neighbors.

The Purpose Of Opportunity Analysis

Opportunity Analysis does several things. First, it identifies an actor's motivations, objectives, capabilities, and perceptions providing Washington with intelligence that can be used to counter or to mitigate a threat. Second, *Opportunity Analysis* can identify a target's weaknesses, and call those weaknesses to the policymaker's attention. And third, *Opportunity Analysis* helps policymakers in policy formulation because it can examine a country's possible reactions to various U.S. policy initiatives.

Before going any further, however, I have to remind the reader that the closer intelligence comes to the policymakers, the greater the chance intelligence analysts will be asked the question, "What should U.S. policy be?" Remember that by law the Intelligence Community cannot make policy and intelligence analysts should never tell policymakers what policy should be.

For those of us who are or have been intelligence analysts, we may see what we think policy should be, but we must never give in to the temptation to articulate those thoughts. There are a number of pitfalls.

First, if you do tell a member of the policymaking community what policy should be and it proves to be correct, you will never get credit. Second, if what you see is not correct and the policy fails, you will be blamed for faulty intelligence. You simply cannot win either way. Third, since 9/11, politicians of all stripes have become more willing to cherry pick the evidence for their career or policy gains. These three pitfalls are strong arguments for sticking to analytic tradecraft.

Opportunity Analysis Guidelines

Opportunity Analysis should:

- Be specific in pointing out means and consequences—in other words, how will the target most likely react to a given policy;

- Again, steer clear of prescribing policy;

- Address underlying conditions that encourage opportunity; and,

- Give consequences of any potential reactions.

Opportunity Analysis Tradecraft

As with all intelligence, *Opportunity Analysis* should be:

- Presented in a clear and concise argument;

- Be central to the product's key analytic message (if the Opportunity Analysis is part of a longer project); and,

- Supported by well-researched facts, solid arguments, logical reasoning, and factors driving outcomes.

Short Opportunity Analysis Assertions

Here are some examples of short *Opportunity Analysis* assertions:

- *The growing profile of China's military modernization has prompted greater regional stability concerns and may increase receptivity among China's neighbors to security consultations and cooperation with the US.*

- *A possible short-term solution to disrupt the flow of marijuana from Mexico to the United States is to strategically position resources in key locations in order to interdict and deter continued operations, while the long-term solution is to force traffickers to seek alternative routes and methods by disrupting the smuggling.*

* * *

Opportunity Analysis, then, is an important tool for "actionable intelligence;" it should never be policy prescriptive. *Opportunity Analysis* provides new intelligence or insights that go beyond traditional intelligence products by identifying opportunities to advance U.S. policies. *Opportunity Analysis* can also provide insights into ways to counter or mitigate threats to the U.S. or allied interests.

Chapter 13

Problem Areas

All languages change, but English is the fastest changing language in the world. For example, you now put one space after a period, it is correct to begin an English sentence with an "and" or a "but," and in a number of instances, writers should end sentences with prepositions (the unnecessary preposition, such as "where is it at," is still taboo). Meanings of words are changing. Not too long ago the words "flammable" and "inflammable" were interchangeable. Now, the primary meaning of "flammable" is combustible, while the primary meaning of "inflammable" is a person's temperament or a situation.

When you combine these changes with the fact that in English, a rule is not a rule, it is a suggestion; you quickly understand why well-educated people (including intelligence analysts) periodically have problems with aspects of the language.

In some of my courses I give spelling tests and brief grammar lessons just to help sensitize people to the changes and the problems all of us face who are writers. I tell my students that anyone who earns his or her living by writing should be recertified every five years to ensure correct use of the language.

I was teaching at a major intelligence organization and the head of training took exception to my giving spelling tests. She said all my students had one or more college degrees and the test were insulting. I countered by calling attention that in the class of twelve, one student with an Ivy League degree in aerospace engineering could not put an English sentence together, much less spell. And that another engineer did not know the difference between "their," "there," and "they're." In other words, and unfortunately, a college degree is no guarantee a person knows how to use English correctly.

I believe it is worthwhile to look at some of the problem areas in English that all of us have problems with (note the correct use of a preposition at the end of a sentence). If you have one or more degrees in English, you may want to skim the rest of the chapter or skip to Chapter 14.

Prepositions

I am beginning with prepositions because there are no rules governing them. They are 100 percent idiomatic.

Prepositions are one of the eight basic parts of the English language, but they have no rules. We complicate the problem by using them to change the meanings of our sentences. Look at the following three sentences. I am going to change just one word, the preposition, and want you to think about how your expectations change as to what will follow with each sentence:

- I work *in* an office.

- I work *for* an office.

- I work *at* an office.

Even well-educated, native English speakers get tripped up by prepositions. So, let's take a closer look at some troublesome areas with prepositions.

The Preposition "Up"

The preposition "up" is a good example of all the different meanings prepositions can have when put in prepositional phrases. In fact, "up" may have more different meanings than any other two-letter word in English. Consider the following:

- We look *up* at the sky.

- We wake *up* in the morning.

- At a meeting, we speak *up*.

- At a meeting a topic may come *up*.

- We call *up* a friend.

Idiomatic Expressions Containing Troublesome Prepositions

Correct Idiomatic	Incorrect Idiomatic
accord with	accord to
according to	according with
acquaint with	acquaint to
adverse to	adverse against
aim to prove	aim at proving
among themselves	among one another
angry with (person)	angry at (person)
as regards	as regards to
authority on	authority about
blame me for it	blame it on me
cannot help talking	cannot help but talk
comply with	comply to
conform to/with	conform
correspond to (a thing)	correspond with (a thing)
desirous of	desirous to
graduated from	graduated
identical with	identical to
in accordance with	in accordance to

Correct Idiomatic	Incorrect Idiomatic
in search of	in search for
prefer (one) to (another)	prefer (one) over (another)
prior to	prior than
responsible for/to	responsible on
superior to	superior than
threat of (a subject)	threat to (a subject)
unequal to	unequal for

The Offensive Letter "S"

For some reason the letter "s" seems to have offended those of us living on the East Coast, and we are getting even by using it incorrectly.

The incorrect use of "s" is apparent in two areas. The first is the third person singular of verbs. For example, it is "He goes to the store," not "He go to the store."

I hope you are seated for the other incorrect use of "s." I don't know why, but people are dropping the "s" off plurals. You do not have to be Albert Einstein to recognize that by far the most common way to form a plural in English is to add an "s."

I had one CIA employee give me a sentence that read, "I process 640 invoice a month." At first I thought it was a typo, but then I began seeing similar mistakes over and over again by college educated people. I raised the problem with one of my colleagues at CIA University, and she said all the instructors are seeing this with plurals and the only thing anyone can think of as a reason is text messaging where people take shortcuts.

Words Ending In "S" And "O"

Having said the above about problems with an "s" to form a plural, I have to admit I always had a bit of a problem with making words that end in "s" plural. Is it just an "s" or is it "es?" Here is the general rule: words ending in -ch, x, s or s- like sounds, require an -es for the plural:

- more than one match = matches
- more than one fox = foxes
- more than one gas = gases
- more than one bus = buses (some dictionaries say the plural is busses)
- more than one hiss = hisses
- more than one Jones = Joneses

The use of "es" to form plurals on words ending in "o" is a hold over from earlier forms of English. The following may help you out (it helps me).

The following words must *always* end in "es:"

Singular	Plural
potato	potatoes
echo	echoes
hero	heroes
torpedo	torpedoes
embargo	embargoes
veto	vetoes

The following words are correct both ways, but I am listing the preferred plural first:

ghettos (es)	buffaloes (s)
innuendos (es)	dominoes (s)
mangos (es)	mosquitoes (s)
mottos (es)	tornadoes (s)
zeros (es)	volcanoes (s)
banjos (es)	cargos (es)
halos (es)	flamingos (es)
memento (es)	motto (es)

Now that we have explored the foibles of the letter "s" and words ending in "o', it is time to look at some other problem areas.

The following words ending in "o" should simply add an "s" to form the plurals:

Singular	Plural
Filipino	Filipinos
taco	tacos
sombrero	sombreros
solo	solos
stiletto	stilettos
kimono	kimonos
avocado	avocados
casino	casinos
inferno	infernos
radio	radios
patio	patios
torso	torsos
zoo	zoos

The Lie Versus Lay Problem

The correct use of "lie" and "lay" cause problems, even among well-educated people. I usually think of it this way— animate versus inanimate. For example, I am going to *lie* down and take a nap. You should tell your dog to *lie* down on its bed. But, I am going to *lay* my coffee cup on the table.

Here is chart to help you remember:

	Present Tense	Past Tense	Participle
To recline:	lie, lying	lay	has/have/had lain
To put or place:	lay, laying	laid	has/have/had laid
To tell a falsehood:	lie, lying	lied	has/have/had lied

Examples In The Present Tense:

- I *lie* down for a nap.

- Please don't disturb me; I am *lying* down.

- Hens *lay* eggs.

- I did not *lie* about my job.

- The hen is *laying* eggs.

- I am not *lying* about the facts.

Examples In The Past Tense:

- I *lay* down for a nap at noon yesterday.

- The hen *laid* a dozen eggs in an hour!

- He *lied* on the witness stand.

Examples With A Participle:

- I have *lain* down for a nap every day this week.

- The hen has *laid* eggs three days in a row.

- He has *lied* on the witness stand several times.

The Trouble With Commas —Too Many

The problem with commas is that English has far too many rules—over 300. For reasons known only to grammarians, English allows professions to make their own rules. For example, there are rules for legal English, academic English, intelligence English, and some large corporations set *their own* rules. It is no wonder that people are confused. The use of commas, then, can be something of a comedy skit.

For example, if you are a creative writer, you have probably been taught that in a series of three or more, you do not put a comma before the conjunction at the end. So your sentence would read "The American flag is red, white and blue."

If you are a lawyer or intelligence analyst however, you have to put the comma in so the sentence, in this instance, reads "The American flag is red, white, and blue."

The reason for the latter sentence structure rests in the legal profession's interpretation of grammar. According to legal English, if I have three children and write in my will "I hereby leave all my earthly belongings to Bob, Sally and John," what is Bob's reaction? He will think, "Hot dog, Dad loved me the best, I get half the loot." Without the comma before the "and", Sally and John are equal to Bob and therefore split half the estate. The legal community is tied closely to the Intelligence Community, e.g. the FBI, and state police Fusion Centers. So, intelligence often follows the rules of legal English.

Setting the 300 number aside, let's look at common mistakes.

The Twenty-One Most Common Mistakes In English Sentences

English is a difficult language to use *correctly*. English is continually evolving and changing. Indeed it is the fastest changing of all the Western languages. These characteristics help explain some of the ambiguity in the rules for English and perhaps why we have so many rules.

According to the *Dartmouth University Writing Program*, the following twenty-one mistakes make up 91.5% of the mistakes found in written standard American English.

1. Missing comma after introductory phrases

   For example: After the devastation of the siege of Leningrad the Soviets were left with the task of rebuilding their population as well as the city. (A comma should be placed after "Leningrad.")

2. Vague pronoun reference

   The boy and his father knew that he was in trouble. (Who was in trouble: The boy? His father? Some other person?) Commas need to surround the phrase *and his father.*

3. Missing comma in a compound sentence

   For example: Wordsworth spent a good deal of time in the Lake District with his sister Dorothy and the two of them were rarely apart. (A comma should be placed before the "and.")

4. No Comma In Nonrestrictive Relative Clauses

   Here you need to distinguish between a restrictive relative clause and a nonrestrictive relative clause. Consider the sentence, "My brother in the red shirt likes ice cream." If you have two brothers, then the information about the shirt is restrictive, in that it is necessary to define which brother likes ice cream. Restrictive clauses, because they are essential to identifying the noun, use no commas. However, if you have ONE brother, then the information about the shirt is not necessary to identify your brother. It is non-restrictive and, therefore, requires commas: "My brother, in the red shirt, likes ice cream."

5. Wrong/Missing Inflected Ends

"Inflected ends" refers to a category of grammatical errors that you might know individually by other names— subject- verb agreement, who/whom confusion, and so forth. The term "inflected endings" refers to something you already understand: adding a letter or syllable to the end of a work changes its grammatical function in the sentence. For example, adding "ed" to a verb shifts that verb from present to past tense. Adding an "s" to a noun makes that noun plural. A common mistake involving wrong or missing inflected ends is in the usage of **who/ whom**. "Who" is a pronoun in the subjective case; "whom" is a pronoun with in the objective case. We say, "Who is the speaker of the day?" because "who refers to the **subject** of the sentence. But we say, "To whom am I speaking?" because, here, the pronoun is an **object** of the preposition "to."

6. Wrong/Missing Preposition

Prepositions are difficult because they are idiomatic. Which is better: "different from," or "different than?" Though both are used widely, "different from is considered grammatically correct. The most common distinction between the two is:

Things *differ from* one another.	Toledo is *different from* New York City.
Different than is used to compare.	Today's clothing is *different than* it was thirty years ago.

The same debate surrounds the words "toward" and "towards." Though both are correct, "toward" is preferred in writing. When in doubt, check a handbook. Here are common accepted usages of the two:

Toward means in the direction of a place.	She ran toward home.
Toward indicates attitude toward something.	She is very affectionate toward her children.
Toward indicates the direction of action.	They are heading toward an agreement.
Toward indicates the object of a contribution or partial payment.	The money will go toward helping the family.
Towards means near a period of time.	I always feel hungry towards dinnertime.

7. Comma Splice

A comma splice occurs when two independent clauses are joined only with a comma. For example: "Picasso was profoundly affected by the war in Spain, it led to the painting of great masterpieces like *Guernica.*" A comma splice also occurs when a comma is used to divide a subject from its verb. For example: "The young Picasso felt stifled in art school in Spain, and wanted to leave." (The subject "Picasso" is separated from one of its verbs "wanted." There should be one comma in this sentence, unless you are playing with grammatical correctness for the sake of emphasis—a dangerous sport for unconfident or inexperienced writers.)

8. Possessive Apostrophe Error

Sometimes apostrophes are incorrectly left out; other times they are incorrectly put in (her's, their's, etc.)

9. Tense shift

Be careful to stay in a consistent tense. Too often students move from past to present tense without a good reason. The reader will find this annoying and confusing.

10. Unnecessary shift in person

Don't shift from" I" to "we" or from "one" to "you" unless you have a rationale for doing so.

11. Sentence Fragment

Silly things can be avoided. Unless, like here, you are using them to achieve a certain effect. Remember: sentences traditionally have both subjects and verbs. Don't violate this convention carelessly.

12. Wrong Tense Or Verb Form

People generally understand how to build tenses, sometimes they use the wrong tense, saying, for example, "In the evening, I like to *lay* on the couch and watch TV." "Lay" in this instance is the past tense of the verb, "to lie." The sentence should read: "In the evenings, I like to *lie* on the couch and watch TV." (Please note that "to lay" is a separate verb meaning "to place in a certain position.")

13. Subject-Verb Agreement

This gets tricky when you are using collective nouns or

pronouns and you think of them as plural nouns: "The committee wants (not want) a resolution to the problem." Mistakes like this also occur when your verb is far from your subject. For example: "The media, who *has* all the power in this nation and *abuses* it consistently, *uses* its influence for ill more often than good." (Note that media is an "it," not a "they." The verbs are chosen accordingly.)

14. Missing Comma In A Series

Whenever you list things, use a comma. You'll find a difference of opinion as to whether the next-to-last noun (the noun before the "and") requires a comma. ("Apples, oranges, pears, and bananas ...") *(for intelligence writing always put the comma before the "and.")* Indeed the general advice is to use the comma because sometimes your list will include pairs of things: "For Christmas she wanted books and tapes, peace and love, and for all the world to be happy." If you are in the habit of using a comma before the "and," you'll avoid confusion in sentences like this one.

15. Pronoun Agreement Error

Many students have a problem with pronoun agreement. They will write a sentence like "Everyone is entitled to their opinion." The problem is "everyone" is a singular pronoun. You have to use "his" or "her."

16. Unnecessary Commas With Restrictive Clauses

See point five.

17. Run-On, Fused Sentences

Run-on sentences are sentences that run on forever, they are sentences that ought to have been two or even three sentences but the writer didn't stop to sort them out, leaving the reader feeling exhausted by the sentence's end, which is too long in coming. **Fused sentences** occur when two independent clauses are put together without a comma, semi- colon, or conjunction. For example: "Researchers investigated several possible vaccines for the virus they settled on one."

18. Misplaced Modifiers

Modifiers are any adjectives, adverbs, phrases, or clauses that a writer uses to elaborate on something. Modifiers, when used wisely enhance your writing. But if they are not well- considered—or if they are put in the wrong places in your sentences—the results can be less than eloquent. Consider, for example, this sentence: "The professor wrote a paper on sexual harassment in his office." Is the sexual harassment going on in the professor's office? Or is his office the place where the professor is writing? One hopes that the latter is true. If it is, then the original sentence contains a **misplaced modifier** and should be re-written accordingly: "In his office, the professor wrote a paper on sexual harassment." Always put your modifiers next to the nouns they modify.

19. Dangling Modifiers

Dangling modifiers are a different kind of problem. They intend to modify something that isn't in the sentence. Consider this "As a young girl, my father baked bread and gardened." The writer means: "When I was a young girl, my father baked bread and gardened." The modifying phrase "as a young girl" refers to some noun not mentioned in the sentence. It is, therefore, a dangling modifier. Other dangling modifiers are; more difficult to spot, however. Consider this sentence:

"Walking through the woods, my heart ached."

Is it your heart that is walking through the woods? It is more accurate (and more grammatical) to say, "Walking through the wood, I felt an ach in my heart." Here you avoid the dangling modifier.

20. Its/It's Error

"Its" is the possessive pronoun. "It's is a contraction for "it is."

21. The Wrong Word

Please do not use a word if you have any doubt about its meaning. Do not reach for words to **impress.**

Affect And Effect

I know it may just be me, but "affect" and "effect" always gives me fits. We all have mental blocks when it comes to one or more aspects of English, and this is a big one for me. I always have to stop and think which one to use.

It is difficult to keep "affect" and "effect" straight because they can be either a noun or a verb. But start by remembering this, "affect is almost always a verb and should not be confused with the noun "effect." "Affect" as a verb means to influence or have an "effect" on; as a noun, "affect" means an emotion or emotional response. "Effect" as a verb means to bring about or accomplish; as a noun, "effect" means a result or an influence. The word "affect" is much less used as a noun than a verb.

The Use Of "A" and "An"

The use of the indefinite articles "a" and "an" can be tricky. The general rule is if the next word begins with a vowel (or if you swallow the consonant and go to the vowel) you use "an." In speech, both "a historic occasion" and "an historic occasion" are correct. When using the word "history" or any of its derivatives (history, historical etc.) the rule rests on whether or not the speaker pronounces the "h." In writing, "a historic occasion" is preferred. If the word begins with a consonant, then use "a."

In dealing with an abbreviation, the choice of "a" or "an" will depend on whether you pronounce the expression letter-by-letter or pronounced as a word. Abbreviations that are pronounced letter by letter are called *initialisms*; abbreviations that are pronounced as words are call *acronyms*.

In the following examples, note that when the consonants *F, H, L, M, N, R,* and *S* are pronounced as letters at the start of an initialism, they are preceded by "an."

Pronounced Letter by Letter	Pronounced as a Word
an FBI agent	a FICA tax increase
an HMO physician	a HUD project
an L.A.-based firm	a LIFO method of valuation
an M.B.A. degree	a MASS fund-raising drive
an NAACP member	a NATO strategy
an R.S.V.P.	a RICO investigation
an SRO performance	a SWAT team

When other consonants appear at the start of an initalism or an acronym, they are always preceded by an "a."

a CIA officer	a CARE package
a DUI conviction	a DARE researcher
a MADD parent	a VISTA project
a VOA broadcast	a WATS line

NOTE: To make a parallel construction clear, repeat an article, a preposition, an infinitive, or a pronoun.

Article:	We had a letter and a telegram.
Preposition:	Send the letter to Bob and to Gloria.
Infinitive:	She wanted us to listen and to critique her presentation.
Pronoun:	Give the message to my brother and to my sister.

Problems With Parallelism

One of the frequent complaints made by supervisors of intelligence analysts centers on a lack of parallelism in sentence structure. Faulty parallel occurs when joined parts of a sentence do not have equal grammatical form. Parallelism means that the same parts of a sentence are alike in function and in construction. Take a look at the following examples of correct parallelism:

Subjects	*Ms. Jones* and *Mr. Smith* have finished their meeting.
Verbs	The professor *knew* the subject matter and *presented* it well.
Infinitives	My friend wanted *to see* and *to visit* the museum.
Objects	The man wanted a new *house* and a new *car*.
Indirect object	We will give *him* and *her* tickets to the concert.
Objects of prepositions	The contract is *for him* and *for her*.
Adjectives	*Three efficient* assistants and *two capable* students prepared the class material.
Adverbs	They worked quickly and efficiently.
Phrases	They looked in the closet, under the table, and in the car for the keys.
Dependent clauses	After you get dressed and before you leave for school, please clean up your room
Independent clauses	The letters were written but they were not mailed.

Chapter 14

Improving Your Skills

In this chapter, I would like to pass along some tips for improving intelligence writing. Let's begin by looking at ways to write better intelligence sentences.

Improving Your Sentences

- Avoid starting your topic sentence with a dependent word, phrase, or clause.

- Use simple readable sentences. Simple sentences are easy for the reader to visually digest because they avoid rambling ideas and multiple clauses.

- Keep the average sentence length to 15-17 words.

- Have only one main idea in a sentence.

- If the sentence is too long (25 words or more), see if you can break it into two sentences.

- Now and then, throw in a sentence of five or six words or fewer.

- Use a connective (conjunction) such as "and" or "but" to start a new sentence.

- Long sentences are fine on occasion. Just make sure they are easily understood, flow smoothly, and are punctuated correctly.

- Use proper word order (syntax)

- Make sure the message is the one you intend.

- Keep related parts of a sentence together.

- Try to keep your paragraphs to no more than three or four sentences.

The Dreaded Editor

There is something that stands between the writer and getting the draft into a publishable form. As intelligence analysts we are almost overwhelmed by the data. We spend much of our time down in the weeds because we have to know as much detail and minutia as possible in order to make sense out of what we are dealing with. Remember, we do not have all the facts; we are always dealing with incomplete data.

Abstract diction	speech or writing that makes heavy use of abstract words. Abstract words denote ideas, quantities, emotions or things that exist primarily in the mind and not in the physical world. Avoid abstract diction at all costs.
Ampersand (&)	should only be used in the name of firms such as Smith & Sons Hardware.
Coinage	a word or phrase invented by a writer or speaker. The coining of words is often done by creative writers. The coining of words is how the vocabulary of English or any language grows. Shakespeare is credited with adding dozens of words to the standard English vocabulary. Intelligence analysts should never coin words because there is no set, standard definition of those words. An example of coinage is the teenage girl who described her boyfriend as "a hunkamatic" man.

Concrete diction	speech or writing means using words that refer to tangible or visible things rather than emotions, abstractions, or ideas. For example, "He cried" is clearer than "He felt so sad it brought tears to his eyes." Use concrete diction.
Euphemism	a word or expression used instead of a direct word because the writer or speaker feels the direct word is harsh or coarse. For example, "She passed to her great reward" is a euphemism for "She died." Euphemisms cause problems for intelligence writers because of political correctness and societal speech norms. For example, "collateral damage" is a particularly annoying euphemism for "civilian casualties." Another euphemism that is intended to obscure is "armed intervention" for "invade." As irritating as these euphemisms are, they do find their way into intelligence and crime. Wherever possible try to avoid euphemisms because they obscure.
Genteelism	is the first-cousin of euphemisms and is used in preference to a plainer word because the user does not want to seem coarse. An example of a genteelism is "retire" for "go to bed." Do not use genteelisms.

Hyperbole	to exaggerate to make a point. Intelligence and crime analysts never want to exaggerate. Exaggeration undercuts the analyst's credibility and objectivity. An example of hyperbole is to write "A thousand objections were raised at the meeting" when you really mean "A few objections were raised at the meeting."
Metaphor	a figure of speech in which something is spoken of in terms of something else. For example, "Love is a shy flower." Do not use metaphors. They are stock-in-trade for creative writers and poets, not for intelligence and crime analysts.
Simile	similar to a metaphor, only in this case something is said to be like something else. For example, "Love is like a flower." Do not use similes.
Solecism	an error in grammar.
Tone	the manner in which a writer addresses the reader.
Syntax	the arrangement of words to form a sentence. The editor is telling you there is something wrong with the order of the words.

If you are working for an intelligence organization you also have to remember that what you write is not your product, it is the product (and voice) of the intelligence agency you work for. Therefore, you have to be willing to make compromises in words, sentence structure, and style while preserving the integrity of the analysis.

The editor, then, is extremely important and we, the analysts, have to understand their vocabulary. So let's take a few moments and review some of the common words that editors use.

Chapter 15

Questions Intelligence Analysts Should Ask Themselves About The Information In Front Of Them

Intelligence analysts will be wrong a number of times in their careers; it comes with the territory. Remember, we never have all the pieces of the puzzle: we are making judgments on fragmentary information. Even if we did have most or all of the pieces, it is humanly impossible to get it right all the time. Then you throw in the problems I discussed earlier, assumptions and deception, and the magnitude of the problems intelligence analysts face comes into sharper focus.

There are some things all intelligence analysts can do to help lessen the chances of being wrong. For example, he or she can begin by asking the following questions that intelligence analysts should ask themselves about the information and sources they are using. I wish I could take credit for the questions below, but they are taken from lists of questions used to teach intelligence analysts at the federal level:

About The Source:

- What is the source's reliability record, especially on the subject being analyzed?

- What access does the source have?

- What is motivating the source?

  - ✓✓ Money?

  - ✓✓ Politics?

  - ✓✓ Ideology?

  - ✓✓ Revenge ?

- Does the source know the information is going to a federal, state, or city government agency?

- Is the source trying to mislead or deceive?

- Does the source's cultural, ethnic, or religious background influence what he or she is saying? If so, in a positive or negative sense?

- Can you evaluate the sources intelligence?

- What is the source's political, economic, or political expertise?

- Is there any one I can ask about the source?

About The Collector

(Humint often comes from a human source reporting information he or she has heard from someone else.)

- What is the reputation of the collector?

- What is the collector's motivation?

- Does the collector tend to distort or exaggerate?

- Has the collector been coopted by the source or the source's culture. (This is commonly referred to as falling in love with your source.)

- How sophisticated is the collector? (Is he or she being manipulated?)

- What is the collector's technical, economic, or political expertise?

- What is the collector's language ability or cultural knowledge? (If the primary source is not speaking English?)

- Is there anyone I can ask to get more information about the collector?

About The Information

- How accurate do I think the information is?

- How does the information jibe with previous reporting and analysis of the subject?

- How can I corroborate the information?

- Is anything being exaggerated and why?

- What can the adjectives and adverbs being used tell me about the validity of the information?

- Have I questioned every fact?

- What information is missing and what else do I need to know to flesh out what I am reading or being told?

- How can I think creatively about the information?

- Using the information, what scenarios can I brainstorm to gain insights?

- Does the information raise new questions I need to answer?

- Does the information refer to other reporting that could help me?

- What is the motivation of the principal actors in the report and where can I find out more about them?

- How sure does the source seem to be about the accuracy of the information?

- Is the terminology clear?

About The Issue

- Am I seeing all the information that is available?

- Are there sources of information I have overlooked?

- Is there more background I can get?

- Is there information my colleagues can give me?

- Do I need to levy collection requirements?

Words Used to Describe Probability	Degree of Certainity/Uncertainity
Will or is certain	On a scale of 1-10, these terms are 10s. You should use *will* when you can envision no plausble scenario, however remote, where this event will not happen.
Almost certain, Extremely likely.	On the same 1-10 scale, these terms are 9s. There remains some conceivable scenario, although very remote, where this event would not happen.
Highly likely, probable, probably	One the 1-10 scale, these terms are 8s. The degree of uncertainty has expanded slightly, but the probability remains very high.
Likely, probable, probably.	These words are closer to the middle of the 1-10 scale and are 6s or 7s in terms of probability.
Even chance.	This one is clear. It is a 5 on the scale of 1-10. In other words, it is a flip of the coin.
Very Unlikely, highly unlikely, extremely unlikely, little prospect	We are now near the bottom of the scale. Thse words are a 1 on the 1-10 scale. There remains some conceivable scenario, albeit very remote, that this event could happen
No prospects, will not.	We have hit the bottom of the barrel. These words are a 0 on the 1-10 scale. Use them when you can envision no plausible scenario, however remote, that this will happen.

Check List For Supervisors And Analysts

Having said the above, here is a checklist for both supervisors and analysts. Note, there is some repetition between this list and the list above. But repeated checking of these points is invaluable to cutting down on the number of errors that can lead to an intelligence failure. Please note that not all points on the checklist are applicable to all papers. Again please note, the checklist is not original to me, it is pulled from a number of U.S. government agencies' instructional material.

Sources

- Has the analyst considered all relevant reporting—classified and unclassified?

- Did the analyst factor into the analysis the strengths or limitations of the information such as source access, reliability, and age of information?

- Has the analyst conveyed these factors to the reader?

- Has the analyst explained which information proved crucial to particular judgments?

- Has the analyst told the reader about gaps in information for which there are no sources?

Confidence

- Does the analyst express the probability and confidence that he/she assigns to his/her judgments?

- Does the analyst's use of words such as—is, will, may, could—accurately convey the confidence level?

- Has the analyst clearly explained the basis of her/his confidence?

- Has the analyst identified gaps or uncertainties and their significance for her/his judgments and confidence?

- Are the confidence levels consistent with the evidence presented to support them?

Facts Vs. Judgments

- Has the analyst clearly distinguished between intelligence judgments and assumptions?

- Has the analyst made it clear where the reporting ends and the judgments and assumptions begin so that readers can separate facts from assessments?

- Has the analyst explained the implications for his/her judgments if the assumptions are incorrect?

Alternative Analysis

- Has the analyst identified the key counter-arguments, explanations, or viewpoints to main conclusions that would have a significant impact on the reader if they occurred?

- Has the analyst noted the strengths and weaknesses of the alternatives in light of what is known and what is not known?

- Has the analyst used any structured analytic techniques appropriate to the topic?

Relevance

- Can the analyst identify the customer? What are the customer's needs? Does the product help them? Does it give them what they need to do their jobs?

- Does the product go beyond the obvious and present information and analysis that is germane to their operational or policy concerns/needs?

- Has the analyst identified the short-and long-term implications for the customer? Does the analyst address the question, "What can I expect next?"

- Has the analyst identified potential points of leverage that could be used to influence the situation or the actors?

Argumentation

- Are the key analytic points supported by evidence and logic? Are there any inconsistencies or leaps in logic?

- Has the analyst laid the evidence and logic out clearly so readers can easily follow the line of reasoning? Has the analyst structured the paper in the inverted pyramid style? (Main point/ assertion first followed by supporting evidence.)

- Is the language and syntax direct and precise so the reader cannot misinterpret the meaning of the analyst's main point? Can the ideas be conveyed more clearly and succinctly?

- Do graphics, maps, images, and charts effectively illustrate or convey relevant information? Could they be understood even if separated from the text?

Consistency Or Change

- Does the product sustain a previous judgment or advance a new one?

- If it sustains a previous judgment, does it add significant new information or understanding of the issue or problem?

- If it advances a new analytic judgment, does it highlight and explain the change?

- Does it differ from the judgment of another Intelligence Community entity? If so, has this point been called to the reader's attention?

- If this is the first product on this particular issue, has the analyst told the reader of that fact?

Probability

No discussion of improving skills in intelligence analysis and writing would be complete without a brief look at the words used to describe probability. The following is taken from the guidelines on word use as spelled out by the *National Intelligence Estimates*:

1. Will or is certain. On a scale of 1-10, these terms are 10s. You should use will when you can envision no plausible scenario, however remote, where this event will not happen.

2. Almost certain, extremely likely. On the same 1-10 scale, these terms are 9s. There remains some conceivable scenario, although very remote, where this event would not happen.

3. Highly likely, probable, probably. On the 1-10 scale, these terms are 8s. The degree of uncertainty has expanded

slightly, but the probability remains very high.

4.   Likely, probable, probably. These words are closer to the middle of the 1-10 scale and are 6s or 7s in terms of probability.

5.   Even chance. This one is clear. It is a 5 on the scale of 1-10. In other words, it is a flip of the coin.

6.   Low probability, probably not. Here, we have a 2-4 range on the 1-10 scale. The preponderance of events indicates a low probability that this will happen, but it cannot be ruled out.

7.   Very unlikely, highly unlikely, extremely unlikely, little prospect. We are now near the bottom of the scale. These words are a 1 on the 1-10 scale. There remains some conceivable scenario, albeit very remote, that this event could happen.

8.   No prospects, will not. We have hit the bottom of the barrel. These words are a 0 on the 1-10 scale. Use them when you can envision no plausible scenario, however remote, that this will happen.

I would strongly suggest never using the absolutes. If you accept that intelligence analysts are always dealing with fragmentary information and events, how can he or she ever be sure something will or will not happen? Most of your writing will probably employ the words in the middle of the list.

A quick word about words to introduce judgments—every intelligence agency has its own formula. The CIA may say "we believe..," while the FBI might prefer, "the FBI judges…." It is important that you know and use the correct phrase or phrases of your organization.

What We Mean When We Say:

An Explanation Of Estimative Language

(From the Iran National Intelligence Estimate)

We use phrases such as we judge, we assess, and we estimate— and probabilistic terms such as probably and likely—to convey analytical assessments and judgments. Such treatments are not facts, proof or knowledge. These assessments and judgments generally are based on collected information, which often is incomplete or fragmentary. Some assessments are built on previous judgments. In all cases, assessments and judgments are not intended to imply that we have "proof" that shows something to be a fact or that definitively links two terms or issues.

In addition to conveying judgments rather than certainty, our estimative language often conveys 1) our assessment likelihood or probability of an event; and 2) the level of confidence we ascribe to the judgment.

Estimates of Likelihood. Because analytical judgments are not certain, we use probabilistic language to reflect the Community's estimates of the likelihood of developments or events. Terms such as probably, likely, very likely, or almost certainly indicate a greater than even chance. The terms unlikely and remote indicate a less than even chance that an event will occur; they do not imply that an event will not occur. Terms such as might or may reflect situations in which we are unable to assess the likelihood, generally because relevant information is unavailable, sketchy, or fragmented. Terms such as we cannot dismiss, we cannot rule out, or we cannot discount reflect information is unavailable, sketchy, or fragmented. Terms such as we cannot dismiss, we cannot rule out, or we cannot discount reflect an unlikely, improbable, or remote event whose consequences are such that it warrants mentioning. The chart provides a rough idea of the relationship of some of these terms to each other.

Confidence in Assessments. Our assessments and estimates are supported by information that varies in scope, quality, and sourcing. Consequently, we ascribe high, moderate, or low levels of confidence to our assessments, as follows:

High Confidence generally indicates that our judgments are based on high quality information, and/or that the nature of the issue makes it possible to render a solid judgment. A "high confidence" judgment is not a fact or a certainty, however, and such judgments still carry a risk of being wrong.

Moderate confidence generally means that the information is credibly sourced and plausible but not of sufficient quality or corroborated sufficiently to warrant a higher level of confidence.

Low confidence generally means that the information's credibility and/or plausibility is questionable, or that the information is too fragmented or poorly corroborated to make solid analytic inferences, or that we have significant concerns or problems with the sources.

an unlikely, improbable, or remote event whose consequences are such that it warrants mentioning. The chart provides a rough idea of the relationship of some of these terms to each other.

Confidence in Assessments. Our assessments and estimates are supported by information that varies in scope, quality, and sourcing. Consequently, we ascribe high, moderate, or low levels of confidence to our assessments, as follows:

High Confidence generally indicates that our judgments are based on high quality information, and/or that the nature of

Ten Commandments Of Intelligence/Crime Analysts

I recently came across a list of Ten Commandments for intelligence/crime analysts. I was attending a police conference and thought after I read the commandments that they contained a lot of common sense wisdom. So here they are:

First Commandment:

Take the initiative and be aggressive in following you subject and getting your intelligence out.

Second Commandment:

Honor you colleagues and those you work with—remember to give them credit for any input they have in your work.

Third Commandment:

Own the street (for intelligence analysts, own your subject matter or account).

Fourth Commandment:

Know the history of the problem or issue you deal with. Know the culture and background of the people or country you are following.

Fifth Commandment:

Do not ignore evidence—particularly evidence that runs counter to your theses.

Sixth Commandment:

Do not be parochial. Talk, coordinate, and work with other members of the Intelligence Community. No one person or organization has all the right answers.

Seventh Commandment:

Take as much training as possible and if you are a supervisor, see that those you oversee get training.

Eighth Commandment:

Do not be shoved aside. (Yes, intelligence and crime analysts cannot be shrinking violets. They have to have the courage of their convictions without be stubborn.)

Ninth Commandment:

Be credible (I would say be thoroughly knowledgeable about your area of responsibility).

Tenth Commandment:

Never cover-up or shy away from telling the whole and complete truth as your analysis dictates.

Amen!!

Chapter 16

Keys To Good Writing

A few final points before we move to Chapter 17: To be a good writer does not mean just mastering the mechanics of good grammar, spelling and sentence structure. Those three things are central to being a good writer; but good writing, particularly for the work place, is much more than that. To be a successful intelligence analyst and writer, you should remember the following:

Know The Reader's Needs:

You need to *listen* to what is being asked of you and answer the questions being asked. Good writers tell the reader what he/she wants to know. Good writing will also answer the questions the reader may have about the topic you are addressing.

Titles:

Titles are contracts with the reader and should be no more than four or five words. You deliver on the contract in the topic sentence of the first paragraph of your intelligence product. The title and the topic sentence are the hook.

Topic Sentences:

Strong topic sentences are a vital part of good writing. As noted above, topic sentences deliver on the contract you make with the reader. The *initial topic* sentence, then, should capture the main point you are making so the reader will want to read the rest of what you have written.

Subsequent topic sentences should capture the main point of each paragraph.

Organization:

The orderly and logical presentation of information is essential to prevent confusion. Strong topic sentences will aid you in your organization. Indeed, in intelligence writing, unlike other forms of writing, the transition from paragraph to paragraph is from topic sentence to topic sentence, not from the last sentence of a paragraph to the topic sentence of the next paragraph.

Precision Of Language:

I wish I had a pill I could give all of you—swallow the pill and the precise, correct work comes out. Unfortunately, I cannot. That means you have to take the time to choose the word or expression that conveys exactly what you want to say. The crucial test for what you have written is not whether you understand it, but whether the reader has understood your message.

Economy Of Words:

Use clear familiar terms, make each word count, and keep your sentences short. Intelligence writing is concise expository writing. You have to convey your message in as few words as possible—without losing the complexity of your message. No easy task! This does not mean never use long words, but avoid them if a shorter word says the same thing. You should practically eliminate adjectives. Adjectives add color, nuance, innuendo—none of which are part of intelligence writing.

Clarity Of Thought:

Writing is thinking on paper. If your writing is fuzzy or

not well thought out in advance, the reader will get the impression your thinking is flawed. Your written work will be misunderstood.

Active Voice:

Active voice sentences are the preferred sentence structure for most intelligence writing. Active voice is more direct, vigorous, and concise. In active voice, a subject performs an action that an object receives, "Mary bounced the ball." Passive voice either does not identify the actor, or puts the actor after the verb, "The ball was bounced" or "The ball was bounced by Mary." Avoid using passive voice.

Passive Voice:

Passive voice is the preferred sentence structure of some intelligence organizations, specifically those involved in law enforcement. The reason is passive voice is used widely in legal writing. Passive voice allows for greater courtroom argumentation and interpretation. General rules to follow for the use of passive voice are:

- Use passive voice when you do not know who the actor is.

- Use passive voice if you want to emphasize something else in the sentence.

- Do not use passive voice to conceal or hide—the job of an intelligence analyst is to be clear and truthful.

Self-Edit:

Editing and revising are keys to good writing. It is difficult to edit your own work. One approach is to edit it several times. Read your work first for logic, then for spelling and grammar errors, and then for content. Try to give yourself time (a day or two) to edit and put the work aside after each edit. Later, take a fresh look at your work and edit it.

Know The Artforms:

There are many writing "artforms" in the intelligence workplace. They all have their differences. There are differences between memorandums, talking points, executive summaries and other unique templates your office uses. You need to understand the differences and make adjustments in your writing style to accommodate them.

Chapter 17

Problems With Words

Selecting the correct word and using words correctly are vital parts of what we do as intelligence analysts. It is important that all of us select the correct word to convey the meaning we intend. But the English vocabulary can be difficult. English has more words than any other language that are pronounced the same way, may or may not be spelled the same way, and have different meanings. Furthermore, English is not phonetic so that for those of us who are bad spellers, selecting the right word and spelling the word correctly can be a challenge.

The problem is further complicated by the fact that English has the largest working vocabulary of any Western language—800,000 words. French is second with 600,000 and German comes in third at 400,000.

English is also the fastest changing of all the major world languages. In my lifetime some of the words and idioms have changed dramatically. All of us who make our living through the use of words need to be reminded frequently of the correct meanings of words.

Think of the importance of words this way. If you are in military or law enforcement intelligence you may carry a weapon, and you go to the shooting range frequently to hone your skills.

For those of us who write for a living, words are our bullets, and the products we produce are our weapons. We need to practice.

I love words. I keep a file on my laptop of words I come across that I may want to use. When I read, I am always jotting down references to the words in the text. When I complete the book, I go back and add those words or phrases to my file. Words inspire me; words stimulate my thought processes. The list is getting a bit out of hand; it is now over 44 pages. Nevertheless, I periodically read and review this list of words.

The Words	The Correct Usage
A lot, alot, and allot	**A lot:** a considerable amount of something, number or extent and is always written as two words. **Alot:** a misspelling. **Allot:** to distribute or apportion.
About and estimated	Do not use either word to refer to an amount or figure that is stated precisely.
Accede and exceed	**Accede:** to adhere to an agreement. **Exceed:** to surpass.
Accelerate	See **escalate.**
Accidentally	This word is never spelled accidently.
Adapt and adept	To **adapt:** to adjust. **Adept:** to be proficient.
Additionally	**Additionally** should never be used as a transitional expression. Instead, use in addition, moreover, furthermore, besides.
Adverse and averse	**Adverse:** opposed. **Averse:** disinclined.
All ready or already	**All ready:** all set. **Already:** something has taken place.
All right and alright	Make it two words. Alright is incorrect English.
All together and altogether	Use all together for "everyone at the same time" or "all as a group." Use altogether to mean "completely," "entirely," and "wholly."
Amateur and novice	**Amateur:** one who engages in a pursuit, study, science sport as a pastime. **Novice:** one new in the business or in a profession.
Ambivalent and ambiguous	**Ambivalent:** to have mixed feelings. **Ambiguous:** uncertainty or lack of clarity.

The Words	The Correct Usage
Anecdote and antidote	**Anecdote**: a narrative of a particular incident. **Antidote:** a remedy to counteract poison.
And and but	These words are connectives (or conjunctions) and can be used to start a sentence if emphasis is desired.
Anticipate and expect	To anticipate an event typically involves preparing for it, whereas to expect an event usually involves nothing more than waiting for it.
Anymore and any more	**Anymore**: usually an adverb and means "now." Use it only at the end of a sentence to show a negative meaning. **Any more**: used to emphasize something extra.
Army	In addition to the military definition of the word army, it also a group of frogs.
As yet	**Yet** is preferred.
Assume and Presume	If you **assume** something you have nothing to point to, no evidence; to suppose something to be the case without proof. If you **presume** something, you have something you can point to for your belief.
Because	**Because**: used to express an unequivocal cause or reason.
Because of	See due to.
Bemused	**Bemused:** confused or bewildered. It is not synonymous with amused.
Beside and besides	**Beside:** next to. Besides: in addition to.
Biannual and biennial	**Biannual:** twice a year, synonymous with semiannual. **Biennial:** every two years.

The Words	The Correct Usage
Born and borne	**Born:** brought to life. **Borne:** carried.
Boycott and embargo	**Boycott:** refusal to buy or use a particular product or service. **Embargo:** a legal restriction on trade.
Breach and breech	**Breach:** as a noun, is a violation, a gap, or a rift in a solid structure. **Breech:** acceptable only with reference to ordnance and to human anatomy.
Breath, breathe, and breadth	**Breath:** respiration. **Breathe:** to inhale or exhale. **Breadth:** width.
Bring and take	**Bring:** to come forward. **Take:** to go away from.
Calender, calendar, and colander	**Calander:** a machine to make paper or cloth smooth or glossy. **Calendar:** a record of time. **Colander:** a metal or plastic container with a perforated bottom, for draining and straining foods.
Can and may	**Can:** to be able to do something. **May:** to ask permission.
Cannon and canon	**Cannon:** a large gun. **Canon:** a law; a rule; a clergyman belonging to the staff of a cathedral or collegiate church.
Cannot help but	avoid this expression. Use *can only* or *cannot help*.
Censer, censor, and censure	**Censer:** an incense pan. **Censor:** a critic; to criticize. **Censure:** to blame.
Cite, sight, and site	**Cite:** to summon to appear before court, to quote by way of authority or proof, to refer to. **Sight:** a view. **Site:** a place.

The Words	The Correct Usage
Client and customer	**A client:** a person using the services of a lawyer or other professional person. **Customer:** a person who purchases a commodity or service. Both are business patrons.
Coarse and course	**Coarse:** rough or common. **Course:** direction, part of a meal, or a way.
Colleague and partner	**Colleague:** an associate in a profession or a civil or ecclesiastical office. **Partner:** a member of a partnership, joint owner in a business.
Combined and joint	A **combined** exercise involves the forces of more than one country; **a joint** exercise involves two or more services of the same country.
Comprise, compose, and include	**Comprise:** to contain or consist of (e.g., the whole comprises its parts). **Compose:** to constitute or make up (e.g., the parts compose the whole). Use comprise when the reference is to all components; use **include** when the reference is to only some of the components. Do not use comprised of.
Compare and contrast	The appropriate verb/preposition pairings are **compare** to indicate likeness; **compare with** to indicate both likeliness and difference; and contrast with to indicate difference.
Complement and compliment	**Complement:** something that completes; **compliment:** something that flatters or praises.
Connote and denote	**To connote:** to suggest; to **denote:** to mean.

The Words	The Correct Usage
Consist in and consist of	**To consist in:** to lie herein. **To consist of:** to be composed of.
Contact	Avoid in such expressions as *If you have questions, contact 703-111-1111.* Instead you should write *If you have questions, call 703-111-1111.*
Continual, continuous, and continuing	**Continual:** something that occurs intermittently or is repeated at intervals, **continuous** applies to something that is uninterrupted, and **continuing** applies to either case.
Convince and persuade	The two words are not interchangeable. A person is convinced of something after he or she has been persuaded to recognize the need of the legitimacy of the argument.
Council and counsel	**Council:** an assembly or group for conference. **Counsel:** advice, legal adviser.
Critique	Expressions such as to critique a report annoy purists who prefer to review a report.
Decimate	The meaning of this word has changed. Originally it meant one part in every ten. Today, it is accepted to indicate heavy losses. For those of you who are military analysts, however, be careful. Tanks and buildings are damaged or destroyed, not decimated.
Defuse and diffuse	**Defuse:** to remove a fuse from a weapon or to defuse a crisis. **Diffuse:** to spread around or scatter.

The Words	The Correct Usage
Different from, different than, and differs from	**Different from:** correct; **different than:** used to compare. **Differs from:** considered better usage. *Things differ from one another.*
Dilemma	This word refers to a choice between two equally unsatisfactory decisions or courses of action. Do not use it for a simple predicament or a troublesome decision.
Disburse and disperse	**Disburse:** to release funds. **Disperse:** to scatter.
Discreet and discrete	**Discreet:** prudent or judicious. **Discrete:** separate, individual, distinct.
Disinterested and uninterested	To be **disinterested**: to be impartial. **Uninterested**: not interested.
Disqualified and unqualified	**Disqualified:** to render unfit. **Unqualified:** not fit for.
Doubt that and doubt whether	Use **doubt that.**
Due to, because of, and on account of	Due to introduces adjective clauses such as *Her success is due to talent and hard work.* Because of and on account of introduce adverbial phrases such as *He resigned because of ill health.*
Each	As a subject, each takes a singular verb and singular pronoun. If, however, each follows a plural subject, the verb is plural.

The Words	The Correct Usage
Emigrate and immigrate	You **emigrate** from a country. You **immigrate** to a country.
Enthuse	Avoid enthuse in formal documents as a substitute for to show enthusiasm.
Equally as good as	Avoid. Use equally good or as good as.
Equivalent and equal	**Equivalent** indicates qualitative similarity; **equal** indicates precise quantitative likeness.
Escalate, accelerate, and intensify	**Escalate:** to increase by successive stages. Do not use the term to indicate **accelerate** (increase the speed of) or **intensify** (to make more extreme in degree, size, or strength).
Especial and special	**Especial:** exceptional or outstanding. **Special:** distinctive, peculiar, individual, uncommon.
Etc.	Avoid in professional writing. Use such as, and the like, and so on, or and so forth.
Eternity and infinity	**Eternity:** unending time, forever. **Infinity:** unending distance or quantity.
Everyday and every day	**Everyday:** common or ordinary. **Every day:** each day.
Exalt and exult	**Exalt:** to hold someone in high regard; to raise someone to a high standard. **Exult:** to celebrate, to show jubilation.
Except and accept	**Except:** a preposition that takes an objective pronoun. *They invited everyone except Bob and me.* Do not confuse with **accept:** to receive or consent.
Excite and incite	**Excite:** to stir up emotionally. **Incite:** to stir up action.

The Words	The Correct Usage
Exile	A person is exiled from, not exiled to.
Ex-patriots and expatriates	**Ex-patriots** are people who no longer love or support their country. **Expatriates** are people who—although they may love their county—live in another
Extant and extent	**Extant:** still in existence; not extinct. **Extent:** range or size, breath, or scope of something.
Farther and further	Use **farther** for physical measurement. Use **further** for everything else.
Fatal and fateful	**Fatal:** resulting in death. **Fateful:** determined by fate.
Feel, evaluate and feel different	As a verb, **feel** can mean to be aware of something instinctively or emotionally. Analysts, intelligence analysts should evaluate, not feel. As a linking verb, **feel:** followed by an adjective when describing a personal condition—such as I feel bad. *You feel different when your condition has changed from bad to good.*
Fewer and less	**Fewer:** used with things you can count. **Less:** used with things you cannot count.
Fiscal and monetary	**Fiscal** applies to budget issues; **monetary** to money or currency issues.
Flammable and inflammable	**Flammable:** preferred for describing a combustible substance. The primary definition of **inflammable:** a situation or a temperament.

The Words	The Correct Usage
Flare and flair	**Flare as a verb (to flare)**: to blaze brightly; to burst out in anger. **Flair**: natural ability or aptitude; style; flamboyance.
Flaunt and flout	**Flaunt**: to display in a boastful way. **Flout**: to show contempt for; scorn.
Finalize	Most professional writers consider finalize to be pompous and ambiguous. Avoid using it.
Flesh out and flush out	**Flesh out**: to realize, to fill out or to give substance to. **Flush out**: to force an animal or person into the open.
Forceful and forcible	**Forceful**: vigorous, strong, effective. **Forcible** implies or suggests the use of force, often physical violence.
Forego and forgo	**Forego**: to precede in time or place; **forgo**: to do without something.
Fowl and foul	**Fowl**: domestic birds used for food. **Foul**: offensive to the senses.
From among	Avoid. Say or write *choose among the four options*.
Gaffe and gaff	**Gaffe**: a social blunder or an embarrassing mistake. **Gaff**: a large hook on a large pole to land large fish; a pole attached to a ship's mast used to extend a sail.
Gamble and gambol	**Gamble**: to play games of chance; to bet; to take a risk or put at risk. **Gambol**: to skip or leap about playfully; to frolic.
Gourmand and gourmet	**Gourmand**: a lover of food who eats to excess. **Gourmet**: a connoisseur of fine food and drink.

The Words	The Correct Usage
Graduated and was graduated	Both terms are in common use and both should be followed by from.
Grizzly and grisly	**Grizzly:** a grayish North American bear. **Grisly:** causing horror.
Guerrilla and gorilla	**Guerrilla:** a terrorist; a member of a band of volunteer soldiers bent on defeating a more established army. **Gorilla:** a large powerful ape; a thug.
Hangar and hanger	**Hangar:** a building that houses airplanes. **Hanger:** a device used to hang cloths and other items.
Heroine and heroin	**Heroine:** the principal female character in a story. **Heroin:** a highly addictive drug derived from morphine.
Historic and historical	**Historic:** having importance in history. **Historical:** relating to history.
Hoard and horde	**Hoard:** a hidden stock of something, a cache. **Horde:** a large group of people, a crowd.
Hopefully	Is an adverb meaning "full of hope."
Historical and historic	**Historical:** relating to history. **Historic:** having importance in history.
Illicit and elicit	**Illicit:** forbidden by law or custom; unlawful. **Elicit:** to call forth; to draw out; to provoke.
Immerge and emerge	**Immerge:** to submerge or immerge in liquid. **Emerge:** to come forth or to become evident.
Impact	The striking of one body against another, or making a strong, immediate impression. Use impact only as a noun or a transitive verb (e.g. a missile impacts on or in a target area.)

The Words	The Correct Usage
Impermeable and impervious	**Impermeable:** not to allow fluids to pass through. **Impervious:** not affected by. **NOTE:** both words mean impenetrable
Imply and infer:	**Imply:** to hint or suggest. **Infer:** to believe as a result of a hint or suggestion.
Impossible and impracticable	**Impossible:** not possible. **Impracticable:** not possible under present conditions.
In terms of	**In terms of:** fluff and adds little or nothing to your writing. Avoid using the phrase.
Incredible and incredulous	**Incredible:** unbelievable. **Incredulous:** not believing.
Injuries and casualties	Injuries and casualties are suffered or sustained, not received or taken
Interesting	An unconvincing word meant to introduce an idea. It is unnecessary and distracts from the point you are making.
Its and it's	**Its:** the possessive form of it. **It's:** the contraction of it is.
Knot and not	**A knot:** a group of toads. **Knot:** also an interlacing, twining or looping of a cord, rope, or the like, drawn tight into a knob or lump, for fastening, binding, or connecting two cords together or a cord to something else. Knot can also be a grouping of anything. Not: an adverb used to express negation, denial, refusal, or prohibition.
Led	Is the past tense of the verb "to lead."
Lend and loan	**Lend:** a verb. **Loan:** a noun.

The Words	The Correct Usage
Libel and slander	**Libel:** a damaging public statement in print. **Slander:** a damaging public statement made orally.
Lie or lay	**Lie:** to recline. **Lay:** to set something down.
Literally and figuratively	**Literally:** following the exact words, verbatim. **Figuratively:** not the exact words, symbolic.
Main and mane	**Main:** chief. **Mane:** long hair.
Majority and plurality	Avoid these terms if they are not supported by data. The first: more than 50 percent. The second: a group or an individual among three or more who gets the most votes, but still less than 50 percent.
Material and materiel	The pronunciation is nearly the same, but the meanings are very different. The first has a broad meaning. The substance or substances of which things are made; tool or apparatus used for performing a physical task; and something such as an idea or sketch, to be refined and incorporated into a finished effort. The second has a more narrow, specific meaning – the equipment and supplies, such as guns and ammunition, of a military force. It can also mean an organization's equipment and supplies.
May be and maybe	May be: a verb (He may be away next week). **Maybe:** an adverb that: perhaps.
Militate and mitigate	**To militate:** to fight or argue. **To mitigate:** to soften or moderate.

The Words	The Correct Usage
Precipitate, precipitately, precipitant, and precipitous	The first two terms apply to rash or hasty actions. The third is similar, but with a connotation of rushing or falling headlong. Precipitous refers to a physical steepness.
Premier and premiere	**Premier:** a prime minister. **Premiere:** the first performance.
Principal and principle	**Principal:** main or main person. **Principle:** a fundamental idea.
Proactive	**Proactive:** imprecise and is used incorrectly most of the time. It is not a synonym for initiative across the board. **Proactive:** to take the initiative to head off a problem or problems. **Proactive:** acting in advance to deal with an expected difficulty. I would use "initiative" – it is better to say you took the initiative.
Regardless and irregardless	Use regardless. Irregardless: not standard English.
Respectfully and respectively	**Respectfully:** to act courteously. **Respectively:** each in the order given.
Sanction	As a verb, sanction: to grant authoritative permission, approval, and encouragement. As a noun, it: not only approval and encouragement, but also penalty and coercion. Use the word carefully.
Tantamount and paramount	**Tantamount:** equivalent in value, meaning or effect. Paramount: the highest in rank or jurisdiction.

The Words	The Correct Usage
Miner and minor	**Miner:** a worker in a coal mine. **Minor:** lesser in size or someone under legal age.
Momentarily	A fleeting instant; it does not mean at any moment.
Ordinance and ordnance	**An ordinance:** a law, prescribed practice or usage. **Ordnance:** military supplies.
Ought and aught	**Ought:** should. **Aught:** nothing or zero.
Overdo and overdue	**Overdo:** to do too much. **Overdue:** past due.
Packed and pact	**Packed:** crowded. **Pact:** an agreement.
Pair, pare, and pear	**Pair:** two of a kind. **Pare:** to peel. **Pear:** a fruit.
Palate, pallet, and palette	**Palate:** the roof of the mouth. Pallet: a bed or platform. **Palette:** a board holding a painter's paint or a range of colors.
Parameter and perimeter	Mathematicians and scientists use the word **parameter.** Other writers use dimensions or characteristics instead. **Perimeter:** boundary or limits.
Patience and patients	**Patience:** composure or endurance. **Patients:** sick persons.
Plaintiff and plaintive	**A plaintiff:** a party to a lawsuit. **Plaintive:** mournful.
Populace and populous:	**Populace:** the masses or people. **Populous:** thickly settled.
Preclude and prevent	**Preclude:** refers to events. **Prevent** refers to people.
Precede and proceed	**To precede:** to go before. **Proceed:** to begin, to continue.

Chapter 18

Exercises

Here are some exercises you can use to practice the analytic skills outlined earlier in this book. Let's start with a review exercise walking you through the principles used in most Intelligence writing. The first exercise was given to me by an instructor who teaches intelligence analysis for one member of the Intelligence Community. I am using the exercise with his knowledge and permission.

Take a look at it before you do the exercises. Once you read the paragraph below, follow the logic behind the construction of the paragraph as spelled out below the paragraph.

Country "X": Crackdown On Extremists

We believe country "X" has begun a major crackdown on extremists, which the government holds responsible for the campaign of terrorism over the past two years. The Army has been ordered to support the police in cleaning out extremist strongholds, according to special Intelligence. The President of "X" is using last week's attack on a shopping center in a working-class neighborhood to justify calling upon the Army to close down the terrorist campaign, according to a reliable clandestine source. The pro-government press reports the extremists cannot match Army firepower and are taking high casualties. A U.S. Embassy observer reports seeing Army trucks deliver more than 100 prisoners, some badly wounded, to the Central Prison. According to country "X" police officials, these were part of the 1,000 extremists rounded up so far in the crackdown. CIA's Country "X" Terrorism Chronology indicates this the first time the Army has been used against the extremists since the terrorism campaign began in 1993.

Sample Inverted Pyramid Terms Paragraph	Principles and Illustrations
Country X: Crack Down on Extremists	Overall: This inverted pyramid structure begins with the analyst's conclusion (this is the value he adds above the factual reporting). The paragraph then arranges reasoning and evidence (to support the core assertion) in decreasing order of importance. Here the Army's support to police has the most weight so it goes in the second sentence along with the source citation. The remaining sentences are arranged in descending order of importance. There is a logical order as well as a weighing by sequencing. The contextual data in the last sentence is nice to know as an attribution of "first time," but is not as critical to supporting the argument. Many readers will have skipped the less important details, perhaps reading only the first sentence.
We believe country "X" has begun a major crackdown on "extremist elements" which the government holds responsible for the campaign of terrorism over the past two years	A BLUF, or "statement of synthesis", leads the paragraph as a judgment and prediction ("We believe ..."), with a dependent clause to introduce context (two years) that suggests the analytic line and driver. This is the primary analytic conclusion, emphasized by italics.
The Army has been ordered to support the police in cleaning extremist strongholds, according to special intelligence.	Direct information (stated as a fact), with sourcing. It gives direct support for the assertion that a combined crackdown by the police and Army have begun.

Sample Inverted Pyramid Terms Paragraph	Principles and Illustrations
The President of "X" reportedly is using last week's attack on a shopping center in a working-class neighborhood to justify calling upon the Army to close down the terrorist campaign, according to a reliable clandestine source.	Indirect information with sourcing. This statement presents an intentional cause-and-effect pattern that supports the move to close down the extremist campaign.
The pro-government press reports the *extremists* cannot match Army firepower and are taking high casualties.	Sourcing, with indirect information. This suggests the likely success of the Army and government in the crackdown. The characterization of the press as "pro-government" is not supported.
A U.S. Embassy observer reports seeing Army trucks deliver more than fact extends support for a success and for 100 prisoners, some badly wounded, to the Central Prison.	Sourcing, with direct information. This fact extends support for a success and for the crackdown as a government policy.
According to country "X" police officials, these were part of the 1,000 *extremists* rounded up so far in the crackdown.	Sourcing, with indirect information. This suggests the scope of the effort so far, and its likelihood of success.

Sample Inverted Pyramid Terms Paragraph	Principles and Illustrations
CIA's Country "X" Terrorism Chronology indicates this is the first time the Army has been used against extremists since of the terrorism campaign began in 1993.	This is data, or information that has been organized to provide a context for evaluating the likelihood that a matter concern is factual. Data can be direct (a log of events based on observation) or indirect (a chronology based on reports from a liaison intelligence service). Here the crackdown is put in context as unprecedented, and this highlights the Army role.

Exercise #1

DISCUSSION: Here is a review exercise. Remember, an Inverted-Pyramid paragraph presents the main points (or analytic conclusions) at the start. Your argument's conclusion (not the conclusion of the paragraph) is the most general statement of the issue you are exploring, and it leads off, followed by supporting facts, evidence, contextual data, and reasoning. This topic sentence synthesizes and governs everything else in the paragraph, so must not wander or add any information that is not contained in the body of the report. The first point of your report is the best support and any support that follows decreases in evidentiary weight. Thus the paragraph begins with a bang, and ends with a whimper. Do not tell all you know; tell only what your reader needs to know to clearly understand your point.

INSTRUCTION: Arrange the following sentences in the best order to construct a strong analytic paragraph in the Inverted-Pyramid paragraph style. Begin with the most important sentence (the topic sentence) and sequence the rest in declining importance. [This exercise is hypothetical, though similar to the events of July 1990.]

1) The Iraqi health minister this morning appealed to all "patriotic" Iraqi citizens to support the military by donating blood at the local hospitals.

2) In the past two days the Iraqi army has moved 75 percent of its tanks, armored vehicles, and artillery to southern Iraq near the border with Kuwait.

3) The Iraqi air force has placed its forces on alert, and surface-to-air missiles are being moved out of storage facilities to

air bases in southern Iraq.

4) We believe that if President Saddam Hussein gives the order, the Iraqi military could invade Kuwait with little or no advance warning.

5) General Tariq, the Iraqi chief of staff, announced yesterday that all remaining army reserve units are being called to active duty within 24 hours.

(See page 238 for the answer.)

Exercise #2

For my friends and colleagues in Canada, here is a Canadian exercise. Please read the following faux newspaper article on Chinese telecom espionage in Canada and write a paragraph of no more than 125 words. Please use the writing principles outlined earlier in this book.

Canada: Chinese Telecom Espionage

By Claire B. Voiant

Toronto Press

OTTAWA (DATE) *Canada has sent a strong message to the Chinese telecom giant Huawei Technologies telling the company it would block the firm from bidding to build the Canadian government's latest secure telecommunications and email network. The Canadian government is citing a rarely used security protocol to bar the Chinese company.*

The U.S. government has already declared Huawei a threat to national security and recommended its products be barred from all government projects. Canada's national surveillance and cryptology agency, the Communications Security Establishment, has followed suit and warned the military of the security risk of installing Huawei equipment.

The problem with the Chinese company comes at a time when the government in Ottawa is trying to sort out a series of bilateral problems with Beijing on trade and tariff issues. The Canadian government is considering allowing a state-owned Chinese firm to buy a piece of the oil sands and are being encouraged by Beijing to enter into a free trade agreement.

A spokesperson for the Prime Minister said that Ottawa decided to invoke an infrequently used national-security exception that allows it to override trade agreements. The government is concerned about giving the Chinese firm any access to Ottawa's super network: a secure, centralized pipe for e-mail, phone calls, and data.

Ottawa has not said if other companies will be blocked from bidding on the contract, but a government spokesman did say Huawei would be "left out in the cold."

"The government is going to be choosing carefully in the construction of this network," Andrew McFern told reporters during an unrelated press briefing.

Also, on Wednesday, a former top Canadian intelligence official spoke out against Huawei. Specifically, he warned about giving the Chinese firm a foothold in Canada's secure communications system. A former top member of the People's Liberation Army, he noted, founded the company. The company, he said, still maintains strong ties to the state. In response to a question, he refused to rule out that Huawei is a front for Chinese intelligence.

The same former intelligence official cautioned that damage from economic espionage is now on a par with the threat posed by al Qa'ida. "It has become equal to the threat posed by terrorism. Why? It has such long-term repercussions for the future prosperity of Canadians."

Huawei has become an international powerhouse in telecommunications. It has grown in two decades from a small Chinese firm to an international giant, rivaling Sweden's Ericsson as the number one maker of telecommunications equipment in the world. The company has made inroads into Canada's private sector, and it is now supplying equipment to major wireless firms such as Bell and Telus.

Huawei racked up more than $32 billion dollars in sales in 2012. It has 140,000 employees worldwide, including 510 in Canada.

A spokesperson for Huawei rejected any idea that the company has ties to Chinese intelligence or is used in espionage. He also said Huawei has received no signal that it would be barred from bidding for any federal government computer or telecom contract.

Australia recently banned Huawei's Australian unit from bidding on a $38 billion broadband network project, citing the need to protect "national interests."

A Top Secret Canadian government document obtained by this newspaper under the access to information law, indicates that country's security organizations have cast a wary eye on Huawei.

(See page 238 for the answer)

Exercise #3

Please read the following article on the Times Square bombing attack and then write an intelligence paragraph of no more than 75 words.

Times Square Bombing Attack

Faisal Shahzad, the first suspect arrested for involvement in the failed May 1 Times Square bombing attempt, was detained just before midnight on May 3 as he was attempting to depart on a flight from Kennedy International Airport in New York. Authorities removed Shahzad, a naturalized U.S. citizen of Pakistani descent, from an Emirates Airlines flight destined for Dubai. On May 4, Shahzad appeared at the U.S. District Court for the Southern District of New York in Manhattan for his arraignment.

Authorities say that Shahzad is cooperating and that he insists he acted alone. However, this is contradicted by unspecified intelligence sources who claim the attack has international links. On February 3, Shahzad returned from a trip to Pakistan, where, according to a criminal complaint, he said he received explosives training in Waziristan, a key hub of the main Pakistani Taliban rebel coalition, the Tehrik-i-Taliban Pakistan (TTP). Authorities are reportedly seeking three other individuals in the United States in connection with the bombing.

Investigative efforts at this point are focusing on identifying others possibly connected to the plot and determining whether they directed Shahzad in the bombing attempt or merely enabled him. From all indications, authorities are quickly collecting information on additional suspects from their homes and telephone-calls, and this is leading to more investigations and more suspects. While the May attempt was unsuccessful, it came much closer to killing civilians in New York than other recent attempts, such as the Najibullah Zazi case in September 2009 and the Newburgh plot in May 2009. Understanding how Shahzad and his possible associates almost pulled it off is key to preventing future threats.

While the device left in the Nissan Pathfinder parked on 45th street, just off Times Square, ultimately failed to cause any damage, the materials present could have caused a substantial explosion had they been prepared and assembled properly. The bomb's components were common, everyday products that would not raise undue suspicion when purchased—especially if they were bought separately. They included the following:

Some 113 kilograms (250 pounds) of urea-based fertilizer. A diagram released by the US Department of Justice indicates that the fertilizer was found in a metal gun locker in the back of the Pathfinder. The mere presence of urea-based fertilizer does not necessarily indicate that the materials in the gun locker composed a viable improvised explosive mixture but urea-based fertilizer can be mixed with nitric acid to create urea nitrate, the main explosive charge used in the 1993 World Trade Center bombing. (It is not known if the fertilizer in the Pathfinder had been used to create urea nitrate.)

Urea nitrate is a popular improvised mixture that can be detonated by a blasting cap and does require a high-explosive booster charge like ammonium nitrate does; 250 pounds of urea nitrate would be enough to destroy the Pathfinder completely and create a substantial blast effect. If detonated near a large crowd of people, such an explosion could produce serious carnage.

Two 19-liter (5-gallon) containers of gasoline. If ignited, this fuel would have added an impressive fireball to the explosion but, in practical terms, would not have added much to the explosive effect of the device. Most of the damage would have been done by the urea nitrate. Reports indicate that consumer-grade fireworks.

(M-88 firecrackers) had been placed between the two containers of gasoline and were detonated, but they do not appear to have ruptured the containers and did not ignite the gasoline inside them. It appears that the firecrackers were intended to be the initiator for the device and were apparently the source of a small fire in the carpet upholstery of the Pathfinder. This firecracker likely would not have had sufficient detonation velocity to initiate urea nitrate.

Three 75-liter (20 gallon) propane tanks. Police have reported that the tank valves were left unopened, which has led others to conclude that this was yet another mistake on the part of Shahzad. Certainly, opening the tanks' valves, filling the vehicle with propane gas and then igniting a spark would have been one way to cause a large explosion. Another way would have been to use explosives (such as the adjacent fertilizer mixture or gasoline) to rupture the tanks, which would have created a large amount of force and fire since the propane inside the tanks was under considerable pressure. Shahzad may have actually been attempting to blast open the propane tanks, which would explain why the valves were closed. Propane tanks are commonly used in improvised explosive devices (IEDs) in many parts of the world. Even without detonating, the propane tanks would have become very large and dangerous projectiles if the fertilizer had detonated.

That none of these three forms of explosive and incendiary materials detonated indicates that the bomb maker was likely a novice and had problems with the design of the firing chain. While a detailed schematic of the firing chain has not been released, the bomb maker did not seem to have a sophisticated understanding of explosive materials and the techniques required to properly detonate them. This person may have had some rudimentary training in explosives but was clearly not a trained bomb maker. It is one thing to attend a class at a militant camp where you are taught how to use military explosives and quite another to create a viable IED from scratch in hostile territory.

However, the fact that Shahzad was apparently able to collect all the materials, construct an IED (even a poorly designed one) and maneuver it to the intended target without being detected exhibits considerable progress along the attack cycle. Had the bomb maker properly constructed a viable device with these components and if the materials had detonated, the explosion and resulting fire likely would have caused a significant number of casualties given the high density and proximity of people in the area.

It appears that Shahzad made a classic jihadist mistake: trying to make his attack overly spectacular and dramatic. This mistake was criticized by al-Qa'ida in the Arabian Peninsula (AQAP) by leader Nasir al-Wahayshi last year when he called for grassroots operatives to conduct simple attacks instead of complex ones that are more prone to failure. In the end, Shahzad (who was probably making his first attempt to build an IED by himself) tried to pull off an attack so elaborate that it failed to do any damage at all.

The devolution of the jihadist threat from one based primarily on al-Qa'ida the group to one emanating from a wider jihadist movement means that we will see jihadist attacks being carried out more frequently by grassroots or lone wolf actors. These actors will possess a lesser degree of terrorist tradecraft than the professional terrorists associated with the core al-Qa'ida group, or even regional jihadist franchises like the TTP. This lack of tradecraft means that these operatives are more likely to make mistakes and attempt attacks against relatively soft targets, both characteristics seen in the failed May 1 attack.

(See page 239 for the answer)

Answers

David Cariens

Exercise #1

Iraq Poised To Invade Kuwait

We believe that if President Saddam Hussein gives the order, the Iraqi military could invade Kuwait with little or no advance warning. In the past two days the Iraqi army has moved 75 percent of its tanks, armored vehicles, and artillery to southern Iraq near the border with Kuwait. The Iraqi air force has placed its forces on alert, and surface-to-air missiles are being moved out of storage facilities to air bases in southern Iraq. The Iraqi health minister this morning appealed to all "patriotic" Iraqi citizens to support the military by donating blood at their local hospitals. General Tariq, the Iraqi chief of staff, announced yesterday that all remaining army reserve units are being called up.

Exercise #2

Canada Counters Chinese Espionage Threat

The potential threat from China's economic espionage is now on a par with the terrorist threat posed by al Qa'ida, according to a former high-level Canadian intelligence official. To counter the threat, the Canadian government is preparing to ban the Chinese telecom giant, Huawei, from bidding on a contract to build the government's new, secure telecommunications and email system. Government sources in Ottawa say that Canadian Intelligence has had a wary eye on Huawei for some time. Ottawa is invoking a rarely used national security exception to exclude the Chinese firm from the bidding. The U.S. government has already declared Huawei a threat to that nation's national security. The Australian government recently banned Huawei from bidding on a broadband network for national security reasons.

Exercise #3

Al-Qa'ida Attack Exposes Weakness

The failed May 1 Times Square bombing is indicative of an al-Qa'ida trend toward clumsy grassroots or lone wolf terrorist attacks. These single operatives aim for the spectacular, but often lack training and are prone to failure. This lack of tradecraft, does not make al-Qa'ida less a threat, but appears to indicate a weakness in al-Qa'ida's capabilities as it moves away from group-based operations.

Index

D

E

F

G

H

I

U

V

W

Y

About the Author

David Cariens is a retired CIA officer who currently teaches intelligence analysis and writing in the U.S. and abroad. He is the author of *A Question of Accountability: The Murder of Angela Dales* — an examination of the shooting at the Appalachian School of Law in Grundy, Virginia and a textbook, *Critical Thinking Through Writing: Intelligence and Crime Analysis*. Cariens also wrote an analysis of the Virginia Tech rampage entitle, *Virginia Tech: Make Sure it Doesn't Get Out*. He contributed to the International Association of Law Enforcement Intelligence Agency's *Criminal Intelligence for the 21st Century*.

Printed in Great Britain
by Amazon

84620572R00149